SCENES FROM THE PAST 18: RAILWAYS O...

RAILWAYS ALONG THE CLW...

CORWEN

TO

RHYL

via RUTHIN, DENBIGH and St.ASAPH

Ruthin. 22nd April 1957. BR Standard Class 4MT 2-6-4T No.**80086** draws to a halt with the 9.00am from Chester, steam escaping under the cab. Twelve of these locomotives were transferred to Chester during 1956, replacing Stanier design equivalent models. They were not quite as popular as the older designs, the main complaint being the "mangle", or reversing gear control, sometimes referred to as "the bacon slicer". The locomotive ran round it's stock, although it was not unknown for it to be borrowed for a short while in order to replace vans in the Goods Shed. Departure back to Chester was scheduled for 11.44am. Chester men worked the trip throughout, and on returning to the shed would be expected to dispose of their engine before signing off duty.

W.A. Camwell.

BILL REAR

Copyright ©Foxline Publishing and W. G. Rear.
ISBN 1 870119 23 1
All rights reserved
Designed and Edited by Gregory K. Fox
Typeset by Bill Rear, Johnstown, Wrexham
Printed by the Amadeus Press, Huddersfield.

Published by Foxline Publishing
32, Urwick Road, Romiley, Stockport. SK6 3JS

Dedication

During the final preparation of this book, our first grandson, Daniel, arrived. This work is dedicated to him, secure in the knowledge that he will grow up sharing my affection for the railways of North Wales

Eyarth Gorge. 31st August 1961. BR Standard Class 4MT 4-6-0 No.75020 threads through the narrow gorge, safety valves lifting as the train coasts around the sharp curves, heading north to Denbigh and Rhyl with the six coach Land Cruise train from Pwllheli in the penultimate week of working. The loco carried an 89C (Machynlleth) shedplate, but was based at Pwllheli for these workings during the summer months, and worked on regular scheduled turns for the rest of the year. Pwllheli was a sub shed to Machynlleth and engine diagrams were so constructed that they would visit the parent shed every two or three days, and where they received their routine "X" examinations. The carriages in the formation carried roofboards which can be seen on the second and fourth coaches. At this point the line ran parallel to the river and road, the latter at a higher level, where a 30 mph speed restriction sign can be seen behind the fence in front of the house. The following week saw the end of these services forever. Thirty years later, happy memories of trips on these trains is still the subject of conversation amongst non railway enthusiast holiday-makers to the area.

Author's collection.

Contents...

Ruthin. 21st April 1962. BR Standard Class 4MT 4-6-0 No.**75010** waits departure time for the 3.00pm to Chester. This working was Rhyl Loco Diagram Turn No.4 and Enginemen's Turn No.31. However, the loco displays a **"6G"** shedplate, denoting that it was attached to Llandudno Junction shed where it had been a long term resident. Indeed the loco arrived there on 19th September 1953 where it remained until October 1962, apart for eleven days in May 1957 when it moved temporarily to Bangor. It transferred out of the District on 20th October 1962, to Nuneaton. The train stands at the main (Up) platform at Ruthin with the two coach working on a wet Saturday afternoon in 1962, the penultimate week-end of operation before the line finally closed to all passenger services. Latterly few passengers supported the trains, perhaps those shown on the platform were the sole travellers. The station building seems unduly large for a rural line, but it had been constructed with the intention of it becoming the headquarters of the Denbigh, Ruthin and Corwen Railway, an independent concern which struggled for survival for a few years before succumbing to the temptations and protection of the LNWR. From 1953 it became the southern terminus for regular passenger train services, although the line to Corwen remained open for freight and the seasonal Land Cruise workings for another nine years. *Keith Smith.*

Acknowledgements

As usual, this work has been compiled with help and assistance of many people, and without their comments, encouragement, guidance and input, would have been so much harder to complete. Especial thanks are extended to George Sheedy, Vic Thomas and Gus Williams for their help with details of work on Rhyl shed, to R. Glyn Jones, Vernon Roberts, and Vic. Roberts one time members of the staff at Denbigh, and Bob Dennis of Chester. Tony Robinson supplied details of his father, John Robinson, who was appointed Running Shed Foreman at Rhyl in 1947.

Peter Baughan provided valuable information and his books have been an invaluable and authoritive source of reference. Especial thanks must be extended to the staff at Clwyd Record Offices at Hawarden and Ruthin, for facilities provided, and likewise to Gareth Haulfryn Williams of Gwynedd Archives. Richard Strange of Steam Archive Services has ensured that locomotive transfer details are correct, whilst collaboration with Schedules and Working Time Tables has come from Jim Kelly of Ripple Lane depot, Alan Warren and fellow Trustees of The Railway Timetable Archive Trust.

Greg Fox has produced the track plans and drawings to his usual meticulous standard. Alan Simpson of Kirkcaldy and Jim Peden supplied useful information about the Kinmel Park Military Railway.

Eddie Johnson worked his usual wizardry in the darkroom and obtained the best possible prints.

Especial thanks are extended to Norman Jones who spared no expense in time, money and effort to produce prints and transparencies from his collection, as well assisting in countless other ways. Huw Edwards, went to great trouble to provide large scale maps and photographs from his collection.

To Mrs K.M. Platt as usual, for access to her late husband, Geoffrey Platt's photographs and papers. Thanks also to the following for their photographic and other contributions:

Roy Anderson, J.M. Bentley, R.J. Buckley, Colin Caddy, W.A. Camwell, Richard Casserley, (for access to collection of his father, the late H.C. Casserley, Gordon Coltas, John Edgington, Huw Edwards, K. Field, J. S. Gilkes, Norman Kneale, Lens of Sutton, Jim Peden, J.P. Richards, Tony Robinson, Eric S. Russell, Keith Smith, Dave Southern, D. Thompson, Alan Tyson and to Sophia Pari Jones for on-going assistance and encouragement.

Obviously the encouragement and continued support of Greg and Jacqueline Fox, of Foxline Publishing cannot be underestimated, and this, my sixth book in the 'Railways of North Wales' series shows their continued faith.

Finally, to Norma, who, as usual, puts up with disruption, late nights, periods of isolation and changes to her plans without complaining, whilst I am pre-occupied on the computer or away on research, and despite general chaos to her routine, still gives support and encouragement. Without this, the work would have been so much the harder if not impossible.

Bill Rear
Johnstown
June 1993

Ruthin. 21st April 1962. Another look at the 3.00pm train to Chester, shown on the previous page, this time taken from the Down platform. Despite wet conditions and the imminent closure, the platforms are tidy, free of litter and rubbish, the buildings appear in good shape. Behind the camera is a small signal box on the platform, controlling signals and the points to the running lines through the platform roads. Prior to the withdrawal of passenger services to Corwen in February 1953, the Down platform boasted a shelter, part of the stone base of which can be identified at the left hand lower edge of this picture. The footbridge carried a right of way for foot passengers where, prior to the construction of the line to Corwen, was a rough track. The footbridge had an additional branch to the Up platform, although this facility was little used. At one time a goods loop ran behind the platform, but this was severed in 1953, leaving access to the siding off the Down loop, seen beyond the footbridge. Just visible on the Up side across the platform is the stops for the goods warehouse road, and just visible is one of the warehouse stores. *Keith Smith*

CORWEN to RHYL
via
RUTHIN, DENBIGH & St.ASAPH

Corwen. 9th May 1949. Ex Midland Railway Class 3F 0-6-0 No.**43396** was a long time resident of Rhyl shed, usually outstationed at Denbigh for the daily freight turn to Corwen, seen here pulling out of the Up side yard at Corwen with a lengthy train. The station was Western Region property although the London Midland maintained a staff presence here. The practice was for traffic for the LM line was made up by one of the several Western Region Class "K" workings that worked between Ruabon and Bala or Barmouth that paused to shunt at Corwen. At the time of the photograph, the LM were still working passenger services to and from Denbigh, so freight working had to slot in between passenger trains. The Down freight left Denbigh at 9.50am and after a non stop run to Ruthin, proceeded to Corwen, stopping at every station and siding, arriving at 1.06pm. Stock for transfer was put into the Down side sidings and the loco and brake van crossed on to the Up side. They then went on the former shed road to clean the fire and take water. It then coupled on to its train, classified as a "mineral" working and pulled into the platform road to await departure time, which was scheduled for 2.05pm. Because the loco diagram exceeded eight hours, the practice was for the crew who took the freight out to Corwen returned with the 2.25pm passenger to Denbigh, changing footplates with the Denbigh crew working the 12.05pm passenger from there to Corwen, which arrived at the station at 12.54pm. The crews changed footplates on the platform. Once the mineral had cleared the station limits, the passenger drew clear of the Down platform and set back on the Up side, when the loco detached and ran round the stock. Progress for the freight was equally lethargic back to Denbigh, the passenger train overtaking it at Gwyddelwern, and after calling once more at every siding and station on the way, trundled into Denbigh yard at 6.30pm. Traffic over the line at this time was quite heavy, and the train seen here was not untypical. Once passenger services over the line ceased in 1953, the freight train had the line to itself, and the crew worked the freight trip in both directions. *E.S. Russell.*

Historical

Until Edward I drained the estuary of the Clwyd, straightening out the river in the process, to give his castle at Rhuddlan direct access to the sea, the overland journeys to fortifications on the North Wales coast were either from Chester or Shrewsbury. Transport was necessary to supply his garrisons along the Welsh coast and had numerous hazards. Whilst Rhuddlan overlooked the coastal plain, invasion from the hills was not unknown, and smaller castles were established at strategic positions throughout the principality. For several hundred years, Denbigh was the dominant town, guarding the entrance to and from the valley, and administered control over the area, subsequently giving its name to the county. After the Restoration of 1660, the area settled down to concentrate and develop as an agricultural producer, with the principal towns assuming roles as markets, exporting much of their surplus produce by sea until the establishment of stage coach and cartage services. In 1770 there was a suggestion for the construction of a canal from Rhuddlan to Ruthin to serve coal mines which it was proposed to establish in that neighbourhood, although neither coal mines nor canal materialised. The proposal was revived again in 1807, but again unsuccessful.

Denbigh was the hub for the three routes; up the vale of Clwyd to Ruthin and on to Corwen on the river Dee; towards the coast through St.Asaph, and through a gap in the Clwydian Range of hills near Bodfari, to Mold. The establishment of the Chester & Holyhead Railway, which opened to traffic as far as Bangor on 1st May 1848, ensured that the apparent prosperity that followed in the wake of the opening of the main line inspired local communities to consider ways of establishing their own lines. As early as 1845, before its own line was operational, the C&H investigated the possibility of a line from Rhyl to Ruthin, to tap the agricultural traffic, but the project was shelved, due to escalating costs on the main line. Other schemes were mooted, but came to naught.

The Vale of Clwyd Railway

The *Vale of Clwyd Railway* was incorporated by Act of 23 June 1856. The contract to construct was let to David Davies of Llandinam and his partner Thomas Savin. The ceremonial cutting of the first sod was performed by a Mrs Mainwaring at Denbigh on 7th August of the same year. According to reports, construction of the line was fast, for there were few major natural obstacles to overcome. From the start it was assumed that the C&H station at Rhyl would be the northern terminus of the line, but in fact, the VofC Rly had no statutory rights or running powers into the station.

The line as built was single track throughout, with provision made for doubling if traffic justified the expense, which sadly it never did. Connection was made with the C&H at Foryd Junction to the first station at Denbigh, which was a temporary structure, with intermediate stations at Foryd, near the junction, Rhuddlan, St.Asaph and Trefnant. The line was formally inspected by Captain Ross, on 22nd September 1858, but permission to open was initially refused because of unfinished works. These were completed within a week, and the VofC Rly promised to work the line on the 'one engine in steam' principle. A form of train staff operation was proposed, but this was deferred because of the initial low volume of traffic. The contractors obtained ballast from Foryd beach, putting down a branch line across land owned by one of the shareholders, Hugh Robert Hughes of Kinmel Hall, a large landowner in the district and Trustee of the Rhuddlan Marsh Embankment and Commissioner of Her Majesty's Woods, Forests and Land Revenue, who wanted the VofC to terminate at his pier on the west side of the estuary. This proposal was opposed by the CHR which suspected that a fellow VofC director James Napier, who owned the steamer *Lion* which operated between Foryd and Liverpool, believing it would abstract their traffic for Liverpool. As a consequence, Hugh Robert Hughes claimed rights of access to Foryd beach, and took over control of the ballast line, using it for general traffic. The branch connection was severed but interchange took place with the VofC at Foryd station. CHR ejected H.R. Hughes men who promptly went to law and obtained an injunction. By August 1859, the branch was carrying passenger and freight to his pier, where Napier's ship conveyed them to and from Liverpool. Subsequently Napier fell out with the VofC, who wished to establish a separate access to Rhyl, believing that VofC and LNWR negotiations were prejudicial to his steamer operations. A crisis developed among VofC shareholders, when the

Corwen. 24th February 1961. Photographed from the footplate of BR Standard Class 2 2-6-0 No.**78056** pulling past the Down fixed distant signal on the return working to Denbigh. At the foot of the post can be seen the telephone box, which enabled the fireman to establish contact with Corwen East box. Note too the p.way engineer's track at right angles to the running line, just beyond the brake van.   *Norman Jones.*

contractors, Davies and Savin, who held most of the VofC shares obtained as payment for railway works. rejected the lease against the advice of the other directors, whereupon Mainwaring and five others resigned. Robert Gardner from Manchester became the Chairman. By September 1860, the ballast branch was reconnected to the VofC and a Bill was submitted in November for a proper extension, following the original route, together with a proposal from Davies and Savin, for the Rhyl Harbour Bridge & Railway. Ultimately the V.of C. Act of 30th June 1862 authorised the extension which provided an improved junction and a new pier at the terminus. Goods traffic along the harbour branch commenced after the official inspection in August 1864 although permission to run passenger trains was refused because there was no terminal station, signalling or turntable installed. A passenger station was provided north of the level crossing by October 1865 and although Assent to passenger train working was given in 1866, in fact the branch never had a regular passenger service. It survived as a freight only line until 6th April 1959 when the branch was closed.

The Vale of Clwyd purchased three 0-4-2 saddle tank engines from Sharp, Stewart of Manchester. These were No.1 *Clwyd*, No.2 *Elwy* and No.3 *Galtfaenan*, the first two named after local rivers and the third after the Rhyl home of Mr Mainwaring, one of the VofC Rly Co's. directors. Rolling stock was supplied by John Ashbury of Openshaw which consisted of 7 composite carriages, 1 second class carriage, 3 third-class carriages, 2 brake-vans, 1 goods van, 49 goods wagons and 4 timber wagons. Signals were supplied by Stevens & Son and the electric telegraph was completed and put into use at the end of 1862.

The railway formally opened to traffic on 5th October 1858 with four weekday stopping trains. The permanent station at Denbigh came into use in December 1860. The interest shown by the GWR in the nascent DR&C line prompted the LNWR to take control of the VofC, with LNWR directors joining the VofC board in September 1861. The LNWR agreed to work both lines into Denbigh as one undertaking. The LNWR assumed operational control of the VofC in 1864 and The Vale of Clwyd Railway Company was finally absorbed by the LNWR by an Act dated 15th July 1867. 60 goods wagons and three locomotives were taken into LNWR stock.

The Denbigh, Ruthin & Corwen Railway

As mentioned earlier, there had been previous attempts to promote a line through the upper reaches of the vale of Clwyd, including one from Ruabon which broadly followed the course of the line built. Projects for 1859 included the Llangollen & Corwen Railway and the DR&C. Both received Royal Assent on the same date, 23rd July 1860. As with the Vale of Clwyd Railway, the contractors were Messrs Davies and Savin, who put up the money for the Parliamentary deposit, and were rewarded by being appointed the line's contractors despite the fact that their tender for the contract was much higher than any of the others. The first sod was turned by Miss Florence West of Ruthin Castle, on 4th September of the same year. Differences between the contractors caused the partnership to terminate in November, leaving Thomas Savin to wield power on the DR&C board. As an independent concern, the DR&C were courted by the G.W.R., with Savin's support, who saw the opportunity to establish a route to Rhyl. The details of these negotiations are admirably described in Peter Baughan's book *A Regional*

History of the Railways of Great Britain, volume 11, North & Mid Wales. However the LNWR were not prepared to allow the GWR into their territory, and by various means, acquired a controlling interest in the VofC which effectively blocked the GWR's ambitions.

By early 1862 the DR&C had been constructed as far as Ruthin (6¾ miles, and was opened to traffic on Saturday 1st March, operated by the LNWR. Intermediate stations were provided at Llanrhaiadr and Rhewl. The 9¾ mile section of line to Gwyddelwern was passed as satisfactory by Captain Tyler in March 1863. Stations were provided at Eyarth, Nantclwyd and Derwen. This included some heavy earthworks at Eyarth and gradients of 1 in 50 on the climb beyond Derwen to the summit between there and Gwyddelwern. Differences between Savin and the LNWR board delayed the official opening of the section, due to reasons attributed to the former, at odds with his fellow DR&C directors, who wished to lease the line to the LNWR, which was contrary to Savin's own interests. The final 2-mile section from Gwyddelwern to Corwen was not opened until 6th October 1864, with DR&C trains terminating at a temporary station. The ¼ mile extension with connection to the GWR line and their station came into use on 1st September 1865. Savin was

Derwen. 23rd August 1961. The climb from Derwen to the summit of the line before Gwyddelwern was unremitting, with gradients of 1 in 57/50/52 for over a mile after leaving the station, before easing to 1 in 138 for the final mile to the summit, 620 feet above sea level. One of the Rhyl based BR Standard Class 4MT 4-6-0 approaches the 58 chain radius curve shortly before the gradient eases for the final climb, with a Land Cruise working, in the final summer of their working. Note the cleanliness of the ballast, and the vegetation cut back to reduce fire risk. Just visible between the "V" formed by the cutting and between the trees can be seen dust rising from the Craig Lelo Quarries, which provided much of the mineral traffic that sustained the line after withdrawal of passenger services. The train is composed of a variety of passenger stock. *Author's collection.*

declared bankrupt in February 1866 and his control over the DR&C passed back to the board, although Savin had installed nominee directors to look after his interests. Most were ultimately removed from the board by James Ashbury, a shareholder, and Fredrick Adolphus Fynney, solicitor and accountant, in January 1867, and restored relations with Euston, although initially the purge failed to remove the Chairman and his deputy, who were under Savin's influence. By July 1868, the purge was complete and Ashbury had full control. By July 1878 a working agreement with the LNWR came into force, and full vesting into the LNWR was authorised by Act of 3rd July 1877, and taking effect from 1st July 1879. The LNWR acquired eleven coaches, fifty-five freight vehicles, and four locomotives. These comprised two 2-4-0 (formerly LNWR Nos. **2347/2349**) and two 0-6-0 (formerly LNWR **2346/2348**) and apart from No.2348 which remained in LNWR stock until April 1884, were disposed of almost immediately.

The Routes Described.
Corwen to Denbigh.

Station facilities were initially provided by the DR&C at a temporary platform on their own line at Corwen with the commencement of services in the autumn of 1864, until the Corwen & Bala Railway station opened the following year, when the single line from Denbigh was extended, running parallel with the Llangollen & Corwen line into the station. Through booking rights for the GWR, who were responsible for working the Llangollen & Corwen, and the Corwen & Bala lines, the DR&C and subsequently the LNWR - and later the LMS - were safeguarded under various Acts of Parliament. The intermediate station buildings were generally similar in design, with the exception of Derwen. Platforms were of short length and low height. Single line staff token was in use, with the equipment located in the station offices. No signal boxes were provided, other than at Ruthin.

At Corwen, the DR&C line was located on the Up side. Goods traffic to and from the Denbigh line ran through the platform road to the Up-side yard, west of the platform, although passenger trains from Denbigh terminating at Corwen discharged to the Down side platform. The passenger stock was then shunted to the Up side for the return journey. The line, as already mentioned, ran parallel to the Llangollen line for the first ¼ mile before swinging left through ninety degrees, climbing steadily. The railway then crossed the river Dee on a lattice girder bridge of six spans, each of 50ft. Half a mile from the station on the Down side was E. Jones & Sons Bryn Eglwys Siding, served by Corwen bound trains, which set back into the siding to set down or pick up wagons, The siding was listed in the Working Time Tables issued between 1904 and 1947 but traffic had diminished and the entry disappeared from the May 1948 edition. For some unknown reason the siding was not listed in the 1920 or 1956 editions of the RCH Handbook of Stations but was included in the 1929 edition under 'Gwyddelwern'. The climb from Corwen to Gwyddelwern was unremitting, with sections of the line rising at 1 in 58 and 1 in 48 for short stretches, and a half-mile length at 1 in 71. There were also some very severe curves on this section which inhibited Up freight trains immediately on leaving Corwen.

Gwyddelwern station was reached, 2 miles 980 yards from Corwen East Box, the line controlled by a staff token, coloured blue, for the section to Corwen. At one time the station was the southern terminus of the line, and apart from station building, boasted a 'temporary engine shed over the passenger line', which the Inspecting Officer required to be removed before permission to open the line to Corwen was granted. The single platform and station building was on the Down side, with a goods loop on the Up. A small 4 lever frame, controlling signals, was mounted on the platform at the Corwen end. Points were worked by Annetts keys. The 1929 Railway Clearing House Handbook of Stations list the facilities provided for 'goods, passenger, livestock and horses'. There was a small yard on the

Derwen. 23rd August 1961. Taken shortly before the previous picture on the same stretch of line between Derwen and Gwyddelwern, the Land Cruise from Rhyl plods away steadily on the 1 in 52 climb, as the line threads its way between the outcrop of rocks. The open aspect of the countryside shown here is in marked contrast to the previous picture with the scenery changing constantly, and only the rising cloud of dust and steam from the Craig Lelo Quarry pin-point the location precisely. The summit was still some way off, on an easier climb at 1 in 138, but nevertheless it demanded skilled enginemanship on the driver's part, whilst the fireman, who had been kept fully occupied up to this point would soon be able to enjoy a few minutes respite on the descent from the summit to Corwen. After watering the coal in the tender, sweeping the coal dust from the cab floor, and closing the dampers, his time would be spent keeping an eye on the water level, and assisting the driver, looking out for signs of anything amiss on the track or lineside.   *Author's collection.*

Down side at the Denbigh end, with a coal siding and weigh machine, off which a second siding that ran parallel to the main line ended in buffer stops at the short platform ramp. The 25 inch to 1 mile 1901 edition Ordnance Survey map shows an additional siding at the Corwen end that ran behind the platform ramp. Access to the sidings was controlled by small lever frames on the track-side, locked by the train-staff. The siding at the Corwen end was removed between the wars. Interestingly, the District Engineer's Side Strips for 1926 do not show either yard or sidings. The Sectional Appendix for 1937 and 1960 specified that any shunting necessary at the station had to be performed in the loop and not on the main line. The Down starter was renewed during the First World War, replaced by a pre-cast concrete post, which also housed the Up home signal. It is believed that this was one of the first examples of concrete signal posts to be used on the LNWR. Following withdrawal of passenger services on 2nd February 1953, the station remained open for goods traffic until 2nd December 1957.

On departing the station limits towards Denbigh, the single line was resumed, the train staff for the section of line to Nant Clwyd being coloured red. The gradient continued to rise for a further mile until the summit was reached, 620ft above sea level. Beyond the summit were quarries on the Up side connected to the line. These are listed in the Handbook of Stations between Gwyddelwern and Derwen as Craig-Lelo Quarry Co's siding and Dee Clwyd Granite Quarries Co's siding. The side-strip shows the first of these as the Dee Clwyd Granite Quarries Co. who had a single trailing siding served by Denbigh bound trains. A short distance further on was the Craig-Lelo complex, which consisted of a loop, also on the Up side, with sidings parallel to the main line extending off each end of the loop and a second loop off the first. Access to the sidings in both cases was controlled from a ground frame locked by the train staff. Craig Lelo Quarry had their own standard gauge locomotive, a 4 wheel petrol tractor built by Motor Rail in 1925, which was subsequently used on the demolition of the Ruthin to Denbigh section in 1966.

Next station was **Derwen**, 2 miles 1297 yards from Gwyddelwern, which consisted of a single short length low height platform on the Up side. The station buildings were different in design to others between Ruthin and Gwyddelwern, and incorporated a canopy built over the station offices at the Corwen end. Although it was not a staff token station, there was a goods loop on the Down side, which was cut back after regular passenger services ceased, to provide a trailing siding served by Down trains. Although passenger services ceased in February 1953, the station remained open to goods traffic until the line closed completely. The loop was still in place during the summer of 1953. A second trailing siding was located at the Ruthin end of the platform, with a loading wharf. Access to the loop and siding was controlled from two lever ground frames, locked by the train staff. After the loop was severed at the Ruthin end, the track was lifted for about half its length, and rail-built buffer stops installed. The loop was also used as a coal siding until the line closed to all traffic. There were no signals provided after World War II, although it is possible that these had been in place for the opening of the line.

Between Derwen and Nant Clwyd the gradient continued to fall steeply, with a short section at 1 in 73 and longer lengths at 1 in 91. **Nant Clwyd** was 2 miles 121 yards from Derwen, and was a staff

token station with the instruments located in the station office. The short length platform was on the Down side. A goods loop was provided for the commencement of services, but this was removed after passenger services ceased. There was a gated siding on the Down side at the Corwen end of the platform, served by Down trains, which led to a loading bank and coal siding which survived until the line closed, although all other freight traffic apart from coal was discontinued from 2nd December 1957. The platform road at the Ruthin end was extended back beyond the loop point to provide a second siding, with a loading gauge. Points were controlled from two-lever ground frames locked by the train staff. A six lever frame controlled signals. The Handbook of Stations lists the usual facilities plus the ability to load and convey carriages by passenger train. Apart from the removal of the platform canopy, the building remained unchanged until closure. The 1960 edition of the Sectional Appendix however has no reference to the station, and the single line section extended from Gwyddelwern to Ruthin.

Prior to the removal of Nant Clwyd as a staff token exchange point, the next train staff section of line was from Nant Clwyd to Ruthin, and the train staff for this section was coloured blue. The line passed through Eyarth Gorge, about ¾ mile from the station, where road and rail followed the course of the river through spectacular scenery, twisting and turning through extremely sharp curves. A speed restriction was in force through the rock cutting, 20mph for Up trains and 35mph for Down. The cutting marked the first change of gradient since the summit beyond Gwyddelwern, from falling to rising.

Eyarth (3 miles 52 yards) was the next station, and the line through

Derwen. 23rd August 1961. Passing Derwen station, although the platform face and buildings are not visible, the disconnected point rodding and short siding, created when the goods loop was cut back after passenger services over the line ceased in 1953, a reminder of times past. The station was no longer a staff token exchange point, and the slight easing of gradient through the station from 1 in 53 to 1 in 381 enabled drivers to pick up speed before resuming the climb at 1 in 57. Timing over this stretch of line was generous, but nevertheless there was a flexibility afforded by the knowledge that it was extremely unlikely that anyone would be delayed by dropping a minute on the schedule. In any case, time could be regained on the downward descent to Corwen. Another feature that has almost disappeared from the railway scene are the telegraph posts, carrying the S.& T. lines from section to section, and with it has gone the evocative sound of wind in the wires, producing a mournful sound and befitting the bleak landscape. The siding was in regular use, despite the absence of wagons, and the local Coal Merchant's empty lorry can be seen on the private road to the station yard. Presumably he is awaiting a wagon off the daily Class **K** freight.
Author's collection.

the station was located on a slight rising gradient at 1 in 445. A goods loop was located on the Up side and two sidings were situated at either end of the platform ramp off the main line, controlled by the usual two-lever ground frame. The 1929 Handbook of Stations merely lists the facilities as 'Passenger and Goods'. Domestic coal was dealt with from the siding at the Corwen end and the station was listed as open for goods traffic until final closure on the 30th April 1962.

From Eyarth to Ruthin, the line climbed for ¾ mile before levelling out for a quarter of a mile before descending at 1 in 63 to the outskirts of Ruthin, where the fall eased to 1 in 221, then at 1 in 974 through the station, 1 mile 1394 yards from Eyarth.

The single line approached **Ruthin** station passing under Well Street bridge, running in a shallow cutting. Station Road ran parallel to the line as far as the station forecourt, when it swung through ninety degrees and became Market Street. Facilities at the station were more extensive, doubtless cost of constructing the large imposing station building justified as the headquarters of the Denbigh, Ruthin & Corwen Railway Company, according to J.M. Dunn, and as befitted the status of Ruthin as the County town for Denbighshire.

Facilities comprised the station buildings, Up and Down platforms, signal box, a goods warehouse and small yard with public weighbridge facilities. In addition to the normal facilities, the goods department could deal with livestock, including horse and cattle traffic. Coal was also catered for, and the yard offered crane lifting capacity up to three tons. The main platform, buildings and station forecourt were on the Up side, the platform line signalled for 'Up & Down' working, was stated to be 210 yards. The building was of two storey brick construction with a slate roof. A canopy extended over the full width of the platform and for the length of the building, although this was subsequently cut back giving only partial

protection. A large goods warehouse adjoined the platform at the Denbigh end, with the goods yard road access off the forecourt. The yard contained four sidings, made up of a group of three - the centre road of which passed through the warehouse, and a fourth siding running alongside the cattle pens. On the Down side was a second shorter length platform, and only occasionally used for passenger services. The Down loop was 192 yards in length.   An open sheltered area was provided, with a canopy that extended over the full width, and a bench seat, but all this was removed after passenger services to Corwen were discontinued in 1953. A standard LNWR design all wooden 12ft x 8ft signal cabin housing a 22 lever LNWR tumbler frame (15 working) was installed on the platform, which controlled points and signals in the station limits and housed the single line token instruments.   Passengers who detrained on the Down side platform crossed the line by the barrow crossing at the Denbigh end, under the watchful eye of the signalman on duty .A goods loop ran behind the platform and signal cabin, together with a short siding that terminated at the platform ramp. This siding was removed and the goods loop cut back to a siding with access off the Corwen end of the Down side loop line, some time after 1953. A public footbridge crossed the tracks from Market Street at the Corwen end with a second set of steps off the Up side ramp. An engine shed was erected about 1866, and was still in place in 1904 although the Working Time Table for July of that year suggests that it had closed as an operational depot, all traffic over the line by this time being worked from Denbigh or Corwen. No details have yet come to light as to the actual closure date.

The town of Ruthin stands at the southern end of the Vale of Clwyd, at the foot of Llantisilio Mountain, behind which lies Llangollen and the valley of the river Dee. The main line fell at 1 in 135 from Ruthin station, easing after half a mile to 1 in 219 for a further quarter mile before levelling off to beyond Rhewl station. The course of the line

Eyarth. 24th February 1961. The daily freight working from Denbigh to Corwen supplied the wagonload of coal to the local merchants, who depended on the regular and reliable delivery service provided by the railway. Here BR Standard Class 2MT 2-6-0 No. **78056** of Rhyl shed fly-shunts a single wagon back into the siding, whilst the loco grinds to a halt just before the siding point on the main line. The fireman stands by the two lever ground frame, unlocked by the train staff for the section, watching the wagon's progress. Meanwhile the guard will have secured the train from his van and no doubt is in the yard ready to pin down the brakes to check the wagon, should speed be too high. Once the wagon was clear and secure, the fireman would reset the points for the main line once more, and remove the train staff from the frame. The driver would then set back onto the train and after the guard had coupled up, the whole ensemble would continue to Derwen and Corwen. The scene has a timeless air about it, and the only 'giveaway' to progress are the electrification warning 'flashes' on the tender. Note the whitewashed platelayer's hut by the frame. Such structures were commonplace on every line, and today, many survive as a reminder of an age now long gone.
Norman Jones.

was straight, cutting across the valley floor, apart from an 18 chain radius curve on leaving Ruthin station.

Approximately three quarters of a mile beyond the station was Ruthin Lime & Limestone Co, Craig-y-Ddywart Quarry and Works, located on the Up side and about half a mile from the main line, served by freight trains heading towards Ruthin. This traffic persisted until freight services were withdrawn in the 1963, although latterly this was confined to the odd wagon-load as required. This traffic was usually worked to the main line by the quarry's own locomotive, which was, according to the Model Engineer, an 0-4-0 vertical-boilered tank engine, with outside cylinders, until it was scrapped about 1920, replaced by a 4 wheel petrol-mechanical locomotive supplied new, which was re-engined with a diesel power unit in 1956, and which then survived until 1965. A 2ft 0ins. gauge system connected the quarries to the kilns, but no evidence has come to light about motive power used, and wagons may well have been man-handled, or at best horse-drawn from the working face to the kilns. The storage hoppers were located alongside the Ruthin to Denbigh road and discharged into the standard gauge wagons standing on the siding. It was not unknown for a British Railways locomotive, usually the Denbigh trip engine, to work the sidings when the quarry's locomotive was unavailable, and the author recalls seeing Rhyl shed's 3F 0-6-0 No.**43396** standing on the side of the main road, the rails being submerged by lime dust, and at the head of a raft of wagons being loaded.

Rhewl station building and platform were on the Up side, the line running under a minor road bridge. A goods loop, located on the Down side, was rarely used, with a trailing siding on the Up side beyond the passenger platform, which extended to a loading bank, on which a yard crane was mounted. Access to the loop at the north end was controlled from track-side by a 2-lever ground frame locked by the train staff, as was the siding on the Up side. Rhewl level crossing, north of the station, was controlled by signals worked from the 4-lever crossing frame. The station was not designated a passing point and the loop was rarely used. It was lifted after the line closed to passenger traffic in 1962. At one time some passenger protection was provided by a canopy, but this had been removed some years earlier. The station building survives to this day as a private residence, although the minor road overbridge was removed in the 1970's. The station lost its freight traffic from 1st September 1958, but passenger trains continued to call until 30th April 1962 when all services were withdrawn. The station was quite close to the village, and traffic was very supportive. The line maintained roughly a straight course in the centre of the valley for nearly five miles.

Shortly after departing Rhewl, the line resumed a downward gradient at 1 in 130, easing slightly after a further mile to 1 in 136 for 400 yards before levelling out once more, for about half a mile. Just before Llanrhaiadr station was reached, the descent resumed at 1 in 354 and continued beyond the station limits.

The track crossed another minor road before running into **Llanrhaiadr** station, protected by hand operated level crossing gates, in turn protected by signals controlled from Llanrhaiadr station frame, which was a set of five levers mounted on the platform adjoining the crossing gates. Levers 1 and 2 operated the distant and home Up direction signals, lever 3 operated the gate lock, whilst levers 5 and 4 operated the Down direction distant and home signals. The station building was similar in appearance to Rhewl, located on

the Up side. At one time there was a goods loop on the Down side with a trailing siding on the Up, again, similar to Rhewl, but these were removed after the station closed to all traffic on 2nd February 1953 although it remained necessary to have a member of staff on duty to operate the level crossing gates.

The falling gradient resumed for a further mile after leaving the station, firstly at 1 in 148 before easing to 1 in 1042 on a gradual right hand curve of 240 chain radius. Half way into the curve the gradient changed to one rising at 1 in 192 for two hundred yards, then stiffened considerably (by comparison) to 1 in 96 for about a mile. About 1¼ miles from Denbigh the climb eased to 1 in 207 for half a mile, increasing to 1 in 101, then 1 in 69 on a 38 chain radius left handed curve. 200 yards from Denbigh station the gradient eased to 1 in 1073 through the station.

Denbigh station has been described in detail in Scenes From The Past No.15 - The Denbigh & Mold Line - an earlier work in this series, and therefore duplication is considered unnecessary. Throughout the station's existence, station working followed a broadly similar pattern, with Up and Down direction through trains using the main platform; trains from Chester to Corwen ran through the loop line and stopping on the Denbigh to Ruthin section of single line, clear of the points before setting back into the platform, ready for resuming the journey south, if an Up train occupied the northern end

Eyarth. 19th May 1961. The returning daily freight from Corwen approaches Eyarth Gorge, passing over the A494 Ruthin to Corwen road bridge. The river, road and rail compete for space within the narrow confines of the gorge, and which provided the first of many spectacular views that could only be seen from the railway, and whilst the road was at a higher level, vegetation and rocks concealed the view. It is a debatable point whether the view of the line was better from the footplate or from the guard's brake van verandah. Certainly everyone who travelled in the observation coach, when it was attached to the Land Cruise trains commented on the superlative scenery at this point. *Norman Jones.*

of the platform. In such cases, two minutes were allowed for running through the loop line, indicated in the Working Time Tables accordingly. At other times Down trains to Ruthin and Corwen would use the platform road, drawing up to the south end. Usually locomotives took water from the column by No.2. signal box whilst awaiting time. The signalling arrangements were simplified in early 1957 with the commissioning of the new signal box on the Down side, which took over the functions previously undertaken by Mold & Denbigh Junction box, (20 levers), one mile north of the station, at the point where the Vale of Clwyd line parted company with the line to Mold and Chester,Denbigh No 1 signal box, at the north end of the station on the Up side, and Denbigh No.2. box, located at the south end of the main platform again on the Up side. The new box was of modern design,45ft 4ins. x 13ft 0ins, and contained a set of 70 levers L Standard 4½" centre tappet frame. The revised track layout which came into use on the same date dispensed with the separate Up and Down lines between the station and Mold & Denbigh Junction; the former Up line became the Up and Down single track to Foryd Junction, whilst the former Down line became the Up and Down single line to Bodfari. Full details of the changes brought about by the commissioning of the new box were printed in the London Midland Region Western Division *Temporary Speed Restrictions, Permanent Way Alterations, Signalling Alterations, Appendix Instructions* etc. Booklet, W2 No.18 dated Saturday 4th May to Friday 10th May 1957, issued at Crewe by P.J. Fisher, Divisional Operating Superintendent dated 30th April 1957, which lists the full details in Section C of the booklet. Revised single line token instruments were instigated as follows:

DENBIGH - RUTHIN. The staff working between Denbigh No.2. box and Ruthin Token Station has been superseded by Key Token working. The Key Token is triangular in shape, coloured green and lettered **"DENBIGH - RUTHIN"** *and releases the ground frames in section formerly released by the Staff. An auxiliary key token instrument has been provided in the Ticket Collector's Hut at the Ruthin end of Denbigh Station platform.*

The single line between Denbigh station and Bodfari station boxes is worked in accordance with the Electric Token Block Regulations with Key Tokens, square in shape, coloured blue and lettered **"DENBIGH - BODFARI"**.

The single line between Denbigh Station and Foryd Junction boxes is worked in accordance with the Electric Token Block Regulations with Miniature Staffs, round in shape, coloured red and lettered **"DENBIGH - FORYD JUNCTION"** *which releases the ground frames formerly released by the Miniature Staff for the section Mold & Denbigh Junction - Foryd Junction.*

There then follows the changes to operating procedures, points and signals, including specifying the location and re-designated titles to various signal arms. The note continues by stating that :

All the running lines have been provided with (track circuit diamond) signs with certain exceptions.

The L.M.R. internal telephone network for the district, dated August 1957, listed circuit A 303 for offices and stations on the Rhyl to Denbigh Line, although the new Denbigh Station box, with stations, yards and offices on the Denbigh Junction to Mold were on circuit A 310. Chester Control Office to Denbigh was on circuit A1129.It is believed that telephone circuit A1130 covered the Denbigh-Ruthin-Corwen section of line, but at the time of writing was unconfirmed.

Ruthin. 19th May 1961. The daily freight working to Corwen, hauled by ex Midland Railway Class 3F 0-6-0 No.**43618,** seen here from the Guard's van, pulls out of the Down loop line at Ruthin and commences on the single track to the first booked stop at Eyarth. The line threads its way through Ruthin, and naturally enough, the coming of the railway encouraged house building adjoining the line. Station Road is aptly named and runs parallel to the line, on the right hand side of the picture. The course of the trackbed at this point is today (1993) still clearly defined the area having been landscaped and created into a small garden area for part of its length. The freight traffic over the line was dwindling visibly at the time of this photograph, comprising mainly single wagon-loads of coal to local merchants. The 3F was obliged to work tender-first one way, and whilst it was specified that locomotives should work smokebox leading to Corwen on this duty, was not rigidly enforced, as can be seen here. It was frequently a bleak trip with this type of locomotive, the tender providing no shelter, and to be subjected to coal dust, rain and driving wind for nineteen miles and several hours tended to remove the glamour of working on the footplate. On this bright May morning , however, conditions were pleasant for the start of the duty. Notice the 'back-side' of the Up home signal, which is on the outer side of the curve to facilitate its sighting by trains coming from Corwen.   *Norman Jones.*

Denbigh to Rhyl

Between Mold & Denbigh Junction and Trefnant, the section of single line was worked by train staff, coloured blue, and of special make.

Within the station limits but beyond the goods yard on the Up side was a private siding belonging to The Ruthin & Denbigh Tarmacadam Company Ltd, formerly the Denbigh Lime & Stone Co., from the Graig Quarry which made a connection with the shunting neck. Within the quarry itself was a 2ft 0ins gauge tramway, which was abandoned by 1960. At one time there was a 36ft turntable located alongside the quarry siding, but was replaced by larger turntable located behind the Engine Shed on the Down side during LMS days. Until the new Denbigh Station signal box was commissioned in 1957, the running lines north were parallel for the first mile, and which continued to rise on a very slight gradient for a quarter of a mile before starting the gradual descent to the coast. It was worked under absolute block regulations with separate Up and Down lines as far as Mold & Denbigh Junction, near the settlement of Denbigh Green, where a standard LNWR design signal box, to Pattern 'D' stood on the Down side. At this point the track was on level ground. Here, the Mold and Chester line turned east and until 1957 was worked as a double line. The Vale of Clwyd line became single track beyond the junction, with the section of line between Mold & Denbigh Junction and Trefnant, worked by train staff, coloured blue, and of special make. The line continued towards Trefnant with occasional and gradual changes of gradient from falling to rising. At 1 mile 1176 yards from Mold & Denbigh Junction box, the line

ran into **Trefnant** station, where a small goods yard stood on the up side comprising a line to a landing stage and cattle dock, parallel to the running lines, and a second siding with a loop, running at an angle, which terminated close to the goods yard entrance. The yard contained a small crane of 5 ton capacity, and a weighbridge. The Down platform line extended beyond the loop, ending in a headshunt. The platforms were of low height and short length, with the main building on the Up side. This was a two storey square shaped structure of brick construction containing the usual offices with the Station Master's house at the south end. A ground frame of eleven levers stood on the Up platform at the north end controlling the signals in each direction, the loop points and the horse landing connection. The single line token instruments were located in the ticket office. Passengers crossed the line via the road overbridge that stood at the north end of the platforms, and any bulky merchandise off Down trains were transported to the office over the barrow crossing located at the foot of the ramps at the south end of the station. The Down platform itself was latterly devoid of shelter and it is not clear whether there ever was protection provided for passengers bound for Denbigh. The community of Trefnant was clustered around the crossroads, where the Denbigh to St.Asaph road met roads from Mold and Henllan. The station was centrally placed in the village, but traffic was never heavy and the normal staff compliment comprised three persons on each shift, under the overall control of a station master, who lived on the station. It would seem that the freight and parcels traffic played a significant part in the

Ruthin. 10th September 1959. Passenger trains terminating at Ruthin used the main platform on the Up side almost exclusively after the service to Corwen was withdrawn, locomotives running around the stock on the Down platform loop line. The platform remained available as required, but the waiting shelter was removed and there was no protection whatsoever. The former Down goods loop that ran behind the platform was also severed and the section for three quarters of its original length at the Denbigh end lifted. What remained was rarely used, the connection at the Corwen end of the Down loop line remaining, controlled from the signal cabin. Here, the 3.00pm to Chester stands awaiting departure time. During the layover period its locomotive scheduled to shunt the goods yard as required. The daily freight from Corwen has just arrived, pulling into the Down loop, which was signalled for two way working. The fireman can be seen getting off the footplate, single line token in hand, and making for the signal box to hand over the train staff. Once the passenger has cleared the section, the freight continued on to Denbigh. Notice the ornate canopy over the passenger entrance, with the unique design of barge boards which were matched by those adorning the waiting shelter on the Down side. *Norman Jones.*

station's viability, with domestic coal the principal commodity. There was a store on the Up platform, but no goods warehouse. In 1939 and up to the Summer 1948, Passenger Working Time Tables indicated that two minutes were allowed at Trefnant on Rhyl to Denbigh trains for ticket collecting purposes. By September of the same year, the note had disappeared from the 1948 issue and never re-appeared.

Beyond the road overbridge heading north, the tracks converged to single line for the two and a half miles to St.Asaph. The line dipped at 1 in 170 for a quarter of a mile before rising at 1 in 114 for the same distance. A mile from Trefnant was Llanerch Siding, on the Up side of the line. The *Private Sidings Book for 1914* (No.395) indicates an Agreement dated 6th July 1858 between Whitehall Dodd and the Vale of Clwyd Railway Co., and connected the Vale of Clwyd line with Llanerch brick Siding, whose products were used locally at Elwy and Llanerch crossing keepers cottages, and at Trefnant station, amongst others. A second nest of sidings was constructed by the Royal Engineers in the later stages of the Second World War, to service a military stores depot. These sidings gradually fell into disuse, latterly being used for the storage of coaching stock, or supplies of loco coal for Rhyl shed. Its final moment of glory came when the Royal Train was stabled overnight on 10th July 1953, when the Queen visited parts of North Wales following her Coronation. Between Trefnant and St.Asaph the section of single line was worked by train staff, coloured red, and of special make.

The line kept to the western side of the valley and commenced a descent from Llanerch Siding to the coast, at varying degrees of steepness, the approach to St.Asaph station being at 1 in 88, easing through the station to 1 in 422 for three hundred yards or so, before resuming at 1 in 78.

St.Asaph station was located at the upper end and in the older part of the city, close to the cathedral. The main station building and station master's house was on the Up side, and the structure, which still survives in private hands, is an elegant building, in contrast to Trefnant. It was the largest intermediate station on the line, and until the withdrawal of passenger services was a token exchange point where trains could cross. The goods yard was on the Up side, and contained a horse and carriage landing siding parallel with the Up platform, with a 5 ton crane alongside in the yard; a goods warehouse stood in the yard, with a single track passing through the building. A second siding off the warehouse road served as a coal siding. The weigh machine and office stood at the goods yard entrance. Livestock traffic accounted for a high proportion of the freight traffic revenue, and Vale of Clwyd Farmers, an agricultural co-operative association established a depot at the station, and provided the station with a regular income from transport of farm machinery and fertilisers imported, and locally grown agricultural products exported. North Wales Agricultural Engineers also imported implements and machinery. Domestic coal was distributed by several merchants from the yard. In addition, the LMS Country Lorry Service operated from the station yard, covering settlements and villages centred around St.Asaph. After Nationalisation this traffic was retained briefly by the railway, but ultimately passed to the control of British Road Services. Some local milk and fish traffic was handled by the platform staff on a regular basis, and there was a steady income from sundries and small parcels, in addition to the handling of Post Office traffic. Wartime military traffic brought an increase in revenue for the railway, which persisted for a while after the cessation of hostilities.

On the main platform, an open ground frame of 15 levers was located close to the passenger footbridge, which controlled Up and Down signals and the loop and horse landing points. The single line

Llanrhaiadr. April 1962. Llanrhaiadr had its passenger and freight facilities withdrawn on 2nd February 1953, when the services from Ruthin to Corwen were withdrawn. Nevertheless the station remained open for parcels traffic, mainly due to the need to man the hand-operated level crossing gates. These were normally placed across the tracks, and the foot passenger crossing gates were locked by the small lever frame between the road and the station building, bounded off by a timber post, and just visible here. The indicators for the circuit were contained in the wooden box on the side of the building, illuminated by the inevitable oil lamp in what appears to be a non-standard design case. Alongside the lamp housing can be seen the warning bell. At one time a canopy over the platform gave some protection to passengers, but this too was removed after 1953, although its location can be determined from the weathering on the brickwork. Beyond the crossing can be seen cast iron bilingual trespass warning notices, and beyond that the Up Home signal. The course of the line at this point was absolutely straight for some distance in either direction, and staff on duty had excellent visibility in sighting approaching trains. On the far side of the track, immediately beyond the gate can just be seen the gradient board, indicating the track was on level ground towards Ruthin. *Norman Jones.*

token equipment was located in the booking office; the large Webb & Thompson token in use on the section to Trefnant being replaced by miniature ones in 1949. Between St.Asaph and Rhuddlan the section of single line was worked by train staff, coloured blue, and of special make. The Down platform was added in 1877, and boasted a shelter which faced the platform, open to the elements. When passenger services were withdrawn in 1955, the Down loop was removed, although the platform and shelter remained for several years. The line from Rhuddlan crossed over the main A55 road which was built for a single line of track although sufficient land for doubling the line throughout had been provided for. The Rhyl end of the main platform commenced almost at the bridge abutment, hence the need to stagger the Down platform. Passengers crossed the line by an open footbridge which was at the Denbigh end of the platform.

The line resumed singularly towards **Rhuddlan**, the falling gradient stiffening to 1 in 78 for over a mile, where it eased to 1 in 114 for two hundred yards, then again to 1 in 207 for about the same distance, then assuming 1 in 502 for the half mile to Rhuddlan, where it ran into the station limits, passing under the Rhuddlan to Abergele road bridge which straddled the track. A single platform and station buildings were located on the Down side. Although the station was designated a crossing point, with token exchange facilities, the fact is that passenger trains were not permitted to cross here, and this was specified in the Working Time Tables, although a freight train could stand in the Up loop line whilst a passenger train used the platform road. The station buildings were constructed of local brick, and the station master had a house on the site. A wooden goods store was mounted on the platform at the southern end of the platform. A forecourt gave vehicular access to the station, beyond which was the goods yard at the northern end of the site, which contained a cattle dock, horse landing and coal wharf. Four camping coaches were stationed on the site from 1948 and were always well

subscribed. An eight lever ground frame which controlled signals in both directions, together with two points, was mounted on the platform at the northern end of the station building. Between Rhuddlan and Foryd Junction the single line train staff was coloured red.

Freight traffic consisted chiefly of timber and livestock away from Rhuddlan, with domestic coal inward, which was usually handled in the siding alongside the passenger platform.

From Rhuddlan the line resumed single line working to Foryd Junction, the gradient along this stretch being almost level, keeping to the west bank of the river Clwyd for two and three quarter miles. The connection with the Foryd branch and Kinmel Park Private Railway was made at the foot of a short climb where at one time stood Foryd station, which comprised a platform on the down side - together with a station master's house. At one time, a signal box was located here controlling access to the Foryd Pier line. This was located 40 yards north of the Vale of Clwyd line station and consisted of a 15 lever standard LNWR frame. It was replaced by ground frames after 1883. A double line climbed up to Foryd Junction on a 12 chain curve to meet with the Chester to Holyhead main line. Up direction branch trains crossing over the Down main lines to connect with the Up Fast Main, and usually crossed over to the Up Slow Main lines. Down trains for the branch line usually travelled over the Down Slow Main, although a crossover from the fast to the slow lines enabled the branch to be accessed from either main line. Foryd Junction signalbox stood on the Down side in the fork between the branch and the Down Slow main line. The 1910 Register of Signal Boxes gives Foryd Junction frame a total of 56 levers of which 43 were working, although some sources state that the frame consisted of 54 levers.

The Foryd Pier line led off the Vale of Clwyd line and passed under the Chester & Holyhead line, following the west bank of the estuary for 1¼ miles. As mentioned previously, there had been high hopes

Denbigh. 14th July 1954. Western Region engines were occasional visitors to the line, usually engaged on special charter trains from Bala or Dolgellau to Rhyl, conveying parties from the local Sunday Schools on the occasion of their annual pilgrimage to the seaside. In the early fifties, however, enterprising Western Region staff occasionally laid on mid week excursion trains to the coast to cater for the visitor on holiday, and which were very successful, by all accounts. On this occasion, two ex GWR Collett 0-6-0's work south with a return excursion from Bala to Rhyl. Here No.**2292** pilots another member of the same class with ten coaches of LM stock, seen here passing the Up distant for Denbigh. This class of locomotive was not normally resident at Bala, or for that matter, regular performers over the Ruabon to Barmouth line at this time, so presumably these were supplied by Machynlleth (89C) shed which had a large allocation of this type. Bala engine workings were normally provided from Croes Newydd (84J) shed, who had none at this time. In view of the train composition it is possible that the coaching stock for the working was provided by Chester rather than Wolverhampton to cut down Empty Stock working mileage. *Author's collection*

of establishing a passenger station in Rhyl Harbour at Foryd Pier Quay, but these plans came to nought and the branch remained a freight-only line until closure on 6th April 1959. It was a single line from the junction with the Vale of Clwyd line until shortly before the line crossed the Rhyl to Abergele road, where a run round loop line ran parallel, giving the appearance of a double track line. Facilities listed in the RCH '1929 Handbook of Stations' indicate that it was a Goods station. There was one private siding, listed as Jones & Son's Siding. The traffic carried over the line consisted mainly of timber and coal, and in early LMS days the turn only worked on Tuesdays, Thursdays and Saturdays. The daily trip working was restored in the mid 1930's and this frequency continued until closure. The job was designated a Class 'K' freight working, and for most of the time, departed Rhyl about 11.00am taking 15 minutes to reach the pier, including running round the train at Foryd Junction. It remained at the pier for half an hour, undertaking what shunting was necessary, before returning, usually departing just before mid-day. Running round the train at Foryd Junction was repeated, this movement taking place on the Vale of Clwyd branch, under the control of the signalman.

A second branch took off the Vale of Clwyd line, to Kinmel Park camp, a complex set up by the War Office in early 1915, where basic training was undertaken. There are conflicting reports about who constructed the camp. Julian Putkowski in his work 'The Kinmel Park Riots 1919' published in 1989 by Flintshire Historical Society, attributed it to McAlpine, whilst the Birmingham Locomotive Club, in its publication 'Industrial and Independent Locomotives and Railways of North Wales' published in 1969, states that much of the camp was constructed by W. Alban Richards, who used ex M&GNR 4-4-0T No.40 on the job. Probably the most detailed (and accurate) account about the line is to be found in the Industrial Railway Record No.102 published in September 1985 by the Industrial Railway Society, in an article by Philip G. Hindley, who states that various contractors were involved in the camp construction works.Mr Hindley makes no mention of the ex M&GNR loco in his account but does describe in detail, other locomotives known to have worked

on the line either during construction or subsequently under military and private control over the years. Perhaps the best known examples were the ex Shropshire & Montgomery Railway 0-6-2T's *Pyramus* and *Thisbe*. According to Peter E. Baughan, in his work '*A Regional History of the Railways of Great Britain, vol.11, North & Mid Wales*' the first connection between the camp and the main line was made at site of the 1885 **Foryd** Station on the Chester & Holyhead main line in 1915 where it formed a trailing connection with the Down Slow main line. This arrangement must have proved unsatisfactory to the Military and the line was diverted to join the Vale of Clwyd near Foryd Junction on the Foryd Pier line. A deviation to the northern section of line was made in April 1917, provided by the LNWR, with the connection being made first with the Foryd Harbour branch and which was quickly modified to provide through running to and from Rhyl. The line was officially opened for passenger traffic on 14th June 1917 by Sir Pitcairn Campbell, General Officer Commanding-in-Chief of Western Command. Foryd station on the main line was closed on 2nd July 1917 but reopened in July 1919. After cessation of hostilities in 1918, the camp was used to house Canadian soldiers awaiting repatriation, but conditions at the camp were so bad that in early 1919 a series of mutinies broke out, resulting in the deaths of five men on Wednesday, 5th March. The Working Time Table for July 1st 1919 shows a regular service of trains still running between Rhyl station and the camp. A footnote states "*The Kinmel Park Camp Service is worked throughout by the Military Railway*". The Military Authorities cleared and closed the camp as quickly as possible after the mutiny, and for the next few years the line was worked "as required" from Rhyl.

The line was taken over by Lime Firms Ltd. of Llandebie in February 1923, and worked by an associate company - Limestone Products Ltd., of St.George Limeworks, who extended the original Military line to their quarry at St.Georges and worked it as a private siding using their own locomotive, an Avonside built 0-6-0ST named *Margaret*, replaced in May 1960 by a diesel mechanical locomotive. In the early days, according to Mr Hindley, the LMS

Denbigh. 27th August 1954. Until the Denbigh to Rhyl services were withdrawn in September 1955, passengers from the DR&C line for stations on the Vale of Clwyd line were usually required to change trains at Denbigh, effected by crossing over the platform and joining the Rhyl train in the bay. Some workings from the DR&C continued to Chester via Mold, whilst other trains terminated and started from the station, which meant that three trains were required to share two platforms. Whilst not unknown for Corwen trains to work through to Rhyl, it was not normal practice. Here we see the cross platform facilities, with appropriate fingerboards slotted into the post to inform passengers as to which train was which. Notice too the small lever at the base of the post that caused the finger post arms to raise - almost like a rudimentary slotted signal arm and post. The station is sparkling clean, not a scrap of litter to be seen anywhere. Six years after Nationalisation the old style station nameboards remain in place, suitably painted maroon with white lettering, although vitreous enamel totems were suspended under the platform canopy in front of the main building. The tower of the main block gleams white in the background, but the poor internal condition of the building resulted in eventual demolition. *The late Henry C. Casserley.*

worked the original line as far as the level crossing over the St.Asaph to Abergele road. This practice was discontinued during the 1930's when the quarry company took over the working as far as Foryd Junction. Traffic finally ceased in February 1965, the track being lifted two months later. The RCH '1929 Handbook' makes no mention of St.George Quarry as a separate entry but lists the positions of **Kinmel Park Estate** and **The Royal Army Service Corps** under Rhyl - Limestone Products Ltd. Siding, and **Jones & Son's Siding** and **Limestone Products Ltd. Siding** under 'Rhyl and Foryd'. It is believed that Bass Breweries had a depot adjoining the line where it crossed the A55 road, and also made use of the rail facilities in the late 1930's, but this has not been confirmed at the time of writing. After the second world war a timber yard was located alongside the line, which necessitated a spark arrester being fitted to the steam locomotive.

Working the Line
Corwen to Denbigh.

No official Denbigh, Ruthin & Corwen Railway Time Table appears to have survived. However, copy of "Douglas North Wales Railways Time Tables for November 1867", published in Bangor, is deposited in the Ruthin Office of Clwyd Record Services. Details from this publication are reproduced on page 20. Initially the LNWR worked trains between Denbigh and Ruthin, commencing in 1862. The service (worked by the DR&C) was extended to Gwyddelwern (March 1863) and finally to Corwen, first to the temporary platform, (October 1864) which would have inhibited traffic by the necessity to handle on-going freight twice - although this arrangement was only short-lived, then subsequently to the Corwen and Bala station on 1st September 1865. As mentioned elsewhere the LNWR ultimately resumed working of the line with locomotives based at Denbigh, Ruthin and Corwen, although Ruthin shed was out of use by July 1904, the work subsequently divided between the two sheds.

It was the practice for most passenger trains from Corwen to terminate at Denbigh although some workings from the Mold and Chester line were extended to and from Ruthin. All workings were of a local nature, and no through working of coaches took place, although Tranship and Road Vans attached to passenger trains were transferred and worked forward from and to Corwen.

The earliest LNWR time table to hand is a public passenger issue dated January 1875. Trains departed from Corwen at 7.30am to Denbigh, 10.35am through to Chester, 2.40pm to Denbigh and 5.20pm to Denbigh, with additional departures from Ruthin to Denbigh at 8.20am to Denbigh and 2.50pm through to Chester. Three passenger trains worked to Corwen, 7.20am from Chester arriving at 9.55am, 12.00pm from Denbigh due 1.15pm and the 3.40pm from Denbigh due 4.40pm. There were departures for Ruthin at 4.35pm and 7.30pm from Denbigh. The unbalanced working into Corwen was probably offset by a freight working.

It is likely there were two turns based at Corwen, the locomotive being stabled overnight at the GWR shed, with three sets of footplate men and a cleaner. The loco was maintained at Denbigh and changed over daily. Ruthin shed probably had three locomotives and five sets of men based there until the shed closed when the work was shared between Corwen and Denbigh.

The **July 1904** issue of the Working Time Table lists five passenger and one goods arrival at Corwen with the same number of departures. There was an unbalanced conditional Mondays Only goods working between Gwyddelwern and Ruthin. Between Ruthin and Denbigh an additional two passenger, one mixed, one goods (MX) and one Empty Stock (ThSO) trains ran. In the opposite direction, the first train of the day, labelled Empty Carriages and Goods, departed Denbigh at 6.00am for Eyarth. It arrived at Ruthin at 6.55am where the carriages were detached, the goods stock worked forward an hour later, taking five minutes for the two mile journey. It returned to Ruthin at 8.30am and disposed of the freight stock in the yard. The loco then attached to the carriage stock and worked the 8.53am to Corwen returning to Denbigh with the 10.35am working.

After 1904 the pattern of trains remained broadly similar with little variation between the summer and winter workings. The tourist traffic had not really spread beyond the coastal strip and local needs were adequately catered for with five passenger and one freight train daily in each direction. Additional trains ran as far as Ruthin, usually formed by extending the Chester and Mold line trains.

The Chester Engine Diagrams for February 7th **1913** show a through

Denbigh. 1919. An unknown LNWR 2-4-2T pulls away from Denbigh with a train of six wheel stock for Rhyl in the summer of 1919. Notice the original No.1 signal box behind the two arm bracket signal, which survived for another thirty eight years. On the Up side, a raft of cattle trucks stand, hidden behind a brake van and mineral wagon. Agricultural traffic played a major role in the history of the line, of which cattle was the principal commodity, and the yard was frequently full to capacity with this type of wagon. On the Down side an assortment of wagons indicate that the yard was very busy at this time, and indeed it was freight business that provided the last strands of traffic to the town, which outlasted the passenger services by several years.

Author's collection

working for engines and men on the 6.30am passenger from Chester to Corwen, due 9.11am, returning with the 10.30am to Chester, due 12.50pm and worked with a "DX" class locomotive fitted with Automatic Vacuum Brake. 96 miles and 10 hours were booked daily to the engine and men respectively, of No.4. Passenger Link, which consisted of four sets of men. (The driver's daily rate of pay for this link was 7/- (35p). The same link worked two turns between Chester and Denbigh, again with a "DX". The first working was the 8.20am to Denbigh due 9.33am, after which they shunted until 2.00pm. They returned to Chester with the 2.15pm passenger, due 3.26pm, and after disposing of the stock, took the engine on shed where it was re-manned by the second set who worked the 4.37pm to Rhyl, arriving there at 5.44pm. Engine, stock and men then worked the 6.25pm to enbigh due 6.51pm. Loco and men went on shed to turn whilst the stock was worked forward to Ruthin and return by Denbigh men and loco. The Chester men then worked back home via Mold, departing at 9.00pm, due Chester at 10.15pm.

The train services along the line remained broadly the same throughout the First World War, with minor variations in timings. The full working time table for July 1st 1919 for the line is included for reference on page 29.

The formation of the London Midland & Scottish Railway Company in 1923 produced little change in traffic patterns, although the Working Time Table for July of that year now combined the timings into one table whereas formerly the three lines had been displayed separately. There were still five passenger workings in each direction daily, but an additional unbalanced goods now ran daily departing Corwen at 8.15am, through to Mold Junction, where it arrived at 12.55pm. It was worked by Denbigh engine and men, departing at 5.15am as a Class "G" freight as far as Gwyddelwern. It then ran light engine to Corwen where it went on the shed to turn, and

followed after the 8.05am passenger to Chester had cleared the section. It was remanned at Denbigh.

The General Strike of 1926 saw a reduction in the passenger services, the emergency time table for the period show three passenger trains each way between Corwen and Denbigh, with an additional two between Ruthin and Denbigh. It is understood that a freight train ran daily between Corwen and Denbigh. Afterwards traffic reverted to its normal pattern of five passenger trains each way. The following season saw an increase of six passenger trains each way between Corwen and Denbigh, with a further four trains running between Ruthin and Denbigh on weekdays, and an extra train on Thursday and Saturday evenings. There was a change to the method of train operation about this time. Whereas formerly most trains from Chester or Corwen or Rhyl terminated at Denbigh, apart from those which were extended to Ruthin, now most trains from Corwen ran through to Chester, although locomotives and traincrew were changed at Denbigh. In the case of the 8.05am from Corwen, this worked through to Rhyl, and in order to be correctly positioned for passenger interchange, as the main platform was occupied by the 6.52am from Chester to Corwen, ran through the loop on the Down side, for which an extra two minutes were allowed, before setting back into the bay platform.

Freight traffic also took an up-turn and the September 1927 WTT shows three workings daily. From Gwyddelwern a Mineral ran to Mold Junction departing Corwen at 8.18am and arriving at destination at 12.50pm having worked Light Engine to Gwyddelwern,; another Mineral to Denbigh that started in Corwen yard at 2.25pm, arrived at Denbigh 6.32pm, and a Class K Freight which departed Corwen 3.40pm, running Light Engine to Gwyddelwern, finally arriving at Denbigh at 9.15pm. Similarly there were three freight trains daily in the reverse direction, all starting at Denbigh. The first left the yard

Denbigh. 15th August 1961. The LMS Horwich "Crab" 2-6-0 locomotives were not normally associated with trains to Denbigh, and it was equally unusual to find locomotives working tender first from Chester. The engine diagram for this particular working was scheduled for a Chester shed Stanier 2-6-4T. Nevertheless No.42853 from Mold Junction (6B) heads this three coach working, so presumably there had been a shortage of power, or possibly a locomotive failure en route, with the 2-6-0 being substituted at short notice, hence the tender first working. The normal practice would have been to run the locomotive smokebox first and turn on Denbigh turntable prior to the return working. The running lines at this point, north of the shed, are two single lines, namely the Up & Down Denbigh to Foryd Junction, and Up & Down Denbigh to Bodfari, which run parallel from Denbigh Station signalbox as far as the site of the former Mold & Denbigh Junction signalbox, and where the lines diverged. Behind the tender can be seen the line to the turntable road, with its yard lamps protruding above the coaches. Probably the driver and fireman are counting their blessings that the day is fine and dry. Tender first working for a twenty nine mile journey on a locomotive where the tender is narrower than the cab was usually a very uncomfortable experience in wet weather.   *Author's collection.*

at 5.15am and after detaching at Gwyddelwern at 7.25am, ran light engine to Corwen where it turned on the shed before departing back to pick up its train after the first Up passenger had cleared the section. The guard remained with his van at the Craig Lelo Quarry. The daily Down freight left Denbigh at 9.25am and made its leisurely way to Corwen, arriving at 1.00pm (12.30pm on Tuesdays). The third freight left Denbigh yard at 1.25pm and ran to Gwyddelwern where it detached the train and ran Light Engine to Corwen where it turned before returning at 3.40pm to Gwyddelwern.

The closure of the GWR shed at Corwen affected the LMS workings, the latter company being unwilling to take over the shed, and consequently the work was transferred to Denbigh. The pattern of services remained broadly similar. The Passenger Working Time Tables for 8th July to September 22nd **1929** showed a light engine departing Denbigh at 6.55pm, arriving Corwen at 7.45am, to work the 8.08am back to Denbigh, due 8.58am. The stock initially stopped overnight at Corwen, but the WTT dated September 23rd **1929** showed the stock now worked out as the 6.50m passenger and worked back in the same times.

Passenger traffic improved by April **1934** with an extra train running between Corwen and Chester on Fridays and Saturdays only, and a late evening working, departing Rhyl at 9.25pm and 10.25pm as far as Ruthin on Thursdays and Saturdays, the former extended to Corwen (due 10.50pm) on Wednesdays and Saturdays during the holiday season. The stock was worked back empty to Ruthin on Wednesdays, to Denbigh on Saturdays, departing Corwen at 11.10pm. Despite the increase in passenger traffic, by September 1936 the freight traffic had fallen off, and one train each way sufficed. The freight started from Denbigh yard at 9.44am daily, and following a first call at Ruthin Lime Works, called at all stations and sidings, reaching Corwen at 1.00pm. The return journey commenced at

1.45pm and did not arrive back at Denbigh until 6.30pm.

The summer of **1939** was probably the busiest in the line's history, although the basic six trains per day in each direction sufficed, with two additional trains to Corwen on Wednesday and Saturdays, the earlier one returning as a service train on Saturdays, the others as empty stock workings back to Denbigh. There were also eight trains each way between Ruthin and Denbigh on weekdays and an extra one on Saturdays, together with the relevant empty stock workings back to Denbigh. Although there were no Sunday workings over the Ruthin to Corwen section, there were seven passenger workings between Denbigh and Ruthin, and five passenger, one empty stock and one light engine working between Ruthin and Denbigh. Most Sunday workings started or finished at Rhyl. The full working time table is reproduced in the Denbigh & Mold Line book in this series. The freight traffic service remained at one train each way between Denbigh and Corwen and return, in the same approximate timings as in previous years. There was a daily additional train between Denbigh and Ruthin, mainly from Ruthin Lime Works, a further unbalanced working that ran on Thursdays and Saturdays only to Ruthin, and a Tuesdays Only express freight from Ruthin to Denbigh on the first Tuesday in the month, in conjunction with the Cattle Market in the town.

The outbreak of World War Two saw a reduction in services, although the cuts on the DR&C line were not as severe as some branch lines experienced. Four trains ran daily from 11th September, departing Corwen at 8.10am, 10.50am, 6.50pm and 9.10pm. The first worked through to Rhyl, the last to Denbigh, the others working through to Chester. The pattern was unchanged for freight trains during 1940, although some of the timings were slightly different. By October 1940 the passenger service had reverted to five trains daily to Corwen and interestingly, two Saturdays Only workings to

Denbigh. c.1919. One of Denbigh shed's 2-4-2T working bunker first on a six coach set of stock with an Up working, seen here passing the shed. Side views of the building are not very common, but this shows the typical LNWR structure. Other features to note are the line of three plank wagons alongside, which it is believed had contained sleepers for a relaying project in the station yard. Beyond the shed, in the yard, the smokebox from one of the shed's resident 0-6-0 coal engines can be seen. Past the Up side lower quadrant signal is the headshunt for the Graig Quarry siding, which contains a passenger brake coach and other stock. The quarry itself was some half a mile away from the station, and over the years provided a considerable volume of traffic for the line.

Author's collection.

Gwyddelwern, the latter working back to Denbigh as empty stock. There were three trips between Denbigh and Ruthin and return. By October 1943 the Saturdays Only trips to Gwyddelwern had been cut, and in addition to the five trains daily over the line, three trains worked to Ruthin and return during the week and an extra two on Saturdays. The first train out from Denbigh to Ruthin worked as Empty Stock at 5.45am, and the last train on Saturdays from Ruthin, (off the 8.50pm from Rhyl) worked back ECS to Denbigh. This pattern remained broadly similar until the railways were nationalised, passing into the London Midland Region (Western Division) of British Railways.

The summer issue of the working time tables, dated May 31st to September 26th **1948** showed passenger trains daily each way, with a late 9.00pm Saturdays Only train from Rhyl to Corwen, balanced by an empty stock train working to Denbigh. There were three additional workings to and from Ruthin, the first Down and last Up workings run as Empty Stock. The freight train pattern remained at one through working each way, daily, and one afternoon working from Denbigh to Ruthin and back.

The last season of passenger working provided five trains daily each way between Corwen and Denbigh, although by now the evening working from Rhyl had disappeared. Three of the Corwen departures worked through to Chester via Mold, the other two worked through to Rhyl. There were three workings from Ruthin and one empty stock workings back to Denbigh, balanced by the same numbers in the opposite direction. There was an additional train to Ruthin on Saturdays, worked back as ECS afterwards. The one freight working each way remained in the same paths as previously, whilst the afternoon trip from Denbigh to Ruthin became conditional.

Regular passenger services ceased on February 2nd 1953 although the freight working continued as normal.

The following summer saw the normal passenger service cut back, with eleven trains daily between Denbigh and Ruthin, although the workings usually commenced at Rhyl or Chester. There was an increased amount of three-cornered working, whereby a train from Rhyl might work to Denbigh and Ruthin, then work to Chester via Denbigh and Mold, returning to Rhyl along the coast, or at times back to Ruthin and then back through Denbigh and St.Asaph. Some workings were straightforward Chester-Mold-Denbigh-Ruthin and return the same way. The freight trip ran in revised timings, starting and finishing later.

There was little change to the pattern of services until 19th September 1955 when regular passenger services between Rhyl and Denbigh were withdrawn, closure of Denbigh M.P.D. taking place on the same day. There were seven trains daily between Ruthin and Chester, Mondays to Fridays plus one between Ruthin and Denbigh, with an extra train between Ruthin and Denbigh on a Saturday, plus one ECS working on a Saturday evening, balanced by the same numbers of Down workings between Chester, Denbigh and Ruthin. The early morning mail train worked from Rhyl to Ruthin along the Vale of Clwyd line, as did several light engine movements to take up or released from work at Denbigh. Whilst the shed was no longer functional, it was nevertheless still used for short term servicing of locomotives, turning on the turntable etc. Four duties were retained for drivers, nominally attached to Rhyl shed, although no firemen were designated, and staff on firing duties were obliged to travel by bus or on light engines. This arrangement persisted until the Mold line closed to traffic in April 1962.

There were no changes to regular passenger and freight workings during the summer of 1960, and 1961 saw the final summer for the DR&C line, closure notices having been posted before the summer season commenced. Consequently the table was not included in the Working Time Tables, but was included in the supplements, which showed eleven workings each weekday with an extra train late on Saturday from Denbigh to Ruthin. Throughout that summer season there was an air of inevitability about it, once again the Chester and Rhyl to Ruthin time tables were left out of the public and Working tables, although they appeared in supplements. The service remained the same as before, the one freight train to Corwen departing Denbigh about 8.10am, returning from Corwen at 2.10pm, worked by Rhyl men outstationed at Denbigh, designated Rhyl Turn 121. The turn only worked Monday to Friday, and in common with most of the lines under threat, traffic was refused on the slightest pretext, and the locomotives were rarely exerted. Latterly a BR Standard Class 2 tender 2-6-0 performed the work. There was some light engine work to and from Rhyl and the services remained steam worked until final closure. The line remained open to Ruthin after passenger services were withdrawn, mainly for mail traffic, which was usually worked by a Llandudno Junction Class 5 4-6-0. Eventually this was replaced by the diesel locomotive, and Class 24 or 25 Bo-Bo units worked the traffic until final closure.

Denbigh Ruthin & Corwen Railway
November 1867.

Corwen	dep	8.10	10.40	2.50	5.10	7.55	-
Gwyddelwern	dep	8.20	10.50	3.00	5.25	8.05	-
Derwen	dep	8.30	11.00	-	5.35	8.20	-
Nant Clwyd	dep	8.38	11.08	3.25	5.40	8.30	-
Eyarth	dep	8.48	11.18	3.40	5.50	8.42	-
Ruthin	dep	9.00	11.25	4.10	5.55	8.50	-
Rhewl	dep	9.03	11.30	4.13	6.00	8.55	-
Llanrhaiadr	dep	9.10	11.37	4.20	6.05	9.00	-
Denbigh	arr	9.20	11.50	4.30	6.15	9.10	-
Denbigh	dep	-	8.40	12.00	4.00	5.19	9.35
Llanrhaiadr	dep	-	8.50	12.10	4.10	5.25	9.45
Rhewl	dep	-	8.55	12.15	4.15	5.35	9.50
Ruthin	arr	-	-	-	-	-	9.55
	dep	6.15	9.00	12.25	4.20	6.00	-
Eyarth	dep	6.25	9.05	12.32	4.25	6.10	-
Nant Clwyd	dep	6.40	9.15	12.45	4.35	6.30	-
Derwen	dep	6.50	9.22	12.55	4.42	6.40	-
Gwyddelwern	dep	7.15	9.35	1.10	4.52	7.00	-
Corwen	arr	7.30	9.45	1.20	5.10	7.15	-

L.N.W.R. Vale of Clwyd Line.
November 1867.

Denbigh	dep	6.30	9.25	12.05	2.00	4.45	7.52
Trefnant	dep	6.38	9.33	M	2.08	4.53	8.00
St.Asaph	dep	6.45	9.40	M	2.15	5.00	8.07
Rhuddlan	dep	6.55	9.50	M	2.25	5.10	8.17
Foryd	dep	7.03	9.58	M	2.33	5.18	8.25
Rhyl	arr	7.10	10.05	1.00	2.40	5.25	8.32
Rhyl	dep	7.50	11.00	3.00	4.05	7.00	8.40
Foryd	dep	8.00	11.05	M	4.15	7.10	8.50
Rhuddlan	dep	8.07	11.12	M	4.20	7.15	8.55
St.Asaph	dep	8.17	11.22	M	4.27	7.22	9.03
Trefnant	dep	8.27	11.32	M	4.37	7.32	9.13
Denbigh	arr	8.45	11.40	3.55	4.48	7.42	9.20

Note M: Stops all stations on request.

Vale of Clwyd Line
Denbigh to Rhyl

Following Board of Trade inspection on 22nd September 1858, Captain Ross refused permission to open the line on the grounds of some works being incomplete, but which were rectified within the week. The VofC agreed to work the line on the "one engine in steam" principle so the necessary approval was given and the opening of the line between Denbigh and Rhyl, took place on 5th October. The first station at Denbigh was a temporary structure, the permanent building opening two years later. Intermediate stations were provided at Trefnant, St.Asaph, Rhuddlan and Foryd (spelt 'Voryd' at that time). At Rhyl, the VofC ran from Foryd Junction to Rhyl using LNWR metals and used their station by arrangement with the LNWR. The arrangement was probably less than satisfactory and in 1860 the VofC sought powers for a separate rail access to Rhyl via a new bridge. Parliament insisted that in return for the bill getting approval, the LNWR were to be given reciprocal running powers to Denbigh, as well as demanding to see the company's books and the agreement between the Company and its Contractors who had agreed to fund the work. Rather than submit its accounts to scrutiny, the bill was withdrawn.

The first timetable comprised four trains each way, daily, departing Denbigh at 8.50am, 10.25am, 3.35pm and 6.00pm, taking thirty five minutes for the 11¼ mile journey. Return departures left Rhyl at 9.40am, 11.55am, 5.15pm and 8.33pm. There was no Sunday service. Three 0-4-2T locomotives were supplied by Sharp Stewart of Manchester, whilst John Ashbury of Openshaw supplied eleven items of passenger rolling stock. This was found to be inadequate, and further coaches were ordered the following year. As the line prospered more freight rolling stock was needed beyond the original delivery of 53 wagons, one covered van and two brake vans. No details appear to have survived about goods train working over the branch.

No further Vale of Clwyd timetables are available whilst the line remained independent. The LNWR did not include details of the line in its publications until after it had absorbed the smaller company.

The LNWR 1867 public passenger train time table for the Vale of Clwyd line, taken from Douglas *North Wales Railway Time Tables for November 1867* and January 1875 are reproduced.

LNWR. January 1875

DOWN TRAINS Weekdays.							
Denbigh	dep	6.30	9.50	12.10	2.15	4.50	7.50
Trefnant	dep	6.37	9.57	12.17	2.22	4.57	7.57
St. Asaph	dep	6.45	10.05	12.25	2.30	5.05	8.05
Rhuddlan	dep	6.52	10.12	12.32	2.37	5.14	8.12
Foryd	dep	6.59	10.20	12.40	2.44	5.21	8.20
Rhyl	arr	7.05	10.25	12.45	2.50	5.25	8.25

UP TRAINS Weekdays							
Rhyl	dep	7.45	10.55	1.50	4.30	6.15	9.00
Foryd	dep	7.50	10.59	1.54	4.34	6.19	9.04
Rhuddlan	dep	7.56	11.05	2.00	4.42	6.25	9.10
St.Asaph	dep	8.05	11.13	2.09	4.50	6.33	9.19
Trefnant	dep	8.11	11.20	2.22	4.57	6.40	9.27
Denbigh	arr	8.20	11.30	2.29	5.05	6.50	9.35

St.Asaph. August 1960. The Cambrian Radio Cruise pulls away from St.Asaph towards Trefnant and Denbigh with BR Standard Class 4MT No.75034 at the head of a mixed bag of stock. Leading coach is an open brake second coach that was included in the Coronation stock that visited the World Fair in the United States of America in 1939. The former "Club Car" that was included in the formation was incorporated into the second Land Cruise set, slightly modified to make it into an open brake second coach. The lack of corridor gangway at the brake or observation ends inhibited their general return to revenue earning traffic, and the two vehicles were incorporated into the Land Cruise trains almost from the start of the enterprise as a way of recouping their cost. Until 1956 the locomotives used on these workings had been ex LMS Class 2 2-6-0 in the 464xx series, which were ideally suited for this type of work. The Standard BR Class 4 engines that took over the majority of the workings until the Cruises ceased after the 1961 season coped well, although some of the traincrew expressed a personal preference for the smaller engines. *Author's collection.*

The first concrete information on the freight working to hand is found in the July 1904 Working Time Table. Apart from the passenger stations served, the following locations are included:
DOWN TRAINS. (Mileage from Rhyl).
Foryd Pier Junction at 1³/₈ miles. This enabled trains to access the freight line to Foryd Pier, which was worked on an "as required" basis by Down goods trains.
Llanerch Siding at 7½ miles. Served on "as required" basis.
UP TRAINS. (Mileage from Denbigh).
Llanerch Siding. at 3¾ miles.

L.N.W.R. Working Time Table. July 1904

DOWN TRAINS Weekdays

		1	2	3	4	5	6	7	8	9	10	11
		Pass	Goods	Pass	Pass	Pass	Pass	Pass	Cattle	Pass	Pass	Mixed
RHYL	dep	7.50	6.50	9.10	11.00	1.25	3.25	4.40		6.15	8.00	10.25
Foryd Jc.	arr	-	6.55	-	-	X	-	-		-	X	-
	dep	7.52	7.15	9.12	11.02	1X27	3.27	4.42		6.17	8X03	10.28
Foryd Pier Jn												
Rhuddlan	arr	7.57	7.25	9.18	11.08	1.32	3.32	4.47		6.23	8.08	10.34
	dep	7.58	7.35	9.19	11.09	1.33	3.33	4.48		6.24	8.09	10.35
St.Asaph	arr	8.04	7.45	9.25	11.15	1.39	3.39	4.54		6.30	8.15	10.42
	dep	8.06	8.45	9.27	11.17	1.41	3.41	4.56		6.32	8.16	10.44
Llanerch Sdg.			@						C			
Trefnant	arr	8.12	8.55	9.34	11X24	1.47	3.47	5.02	MO	6.39	8.22	10.50
	dep	8.14	9.15	9.36	11X26	1.49	3.49	5.04	5.30	6.44	8.24	10.52
Denbigh Jn.		8.18	9.19	9.42	11.30	1.53	3.53	5.08	5.37	6.48	8.28	10.58
DENBIGH	arr	8.20	9.25	9.44	11.32	1.55	3.55	5.10	5.42	6.50	8.30.	11.01

UP TRAINS Weekdays

		13	14	15	16	17	18	19	20	21	22	23
		Pass	Pass	Pass	Pass	Goods	Pass	Pass	Eng.	Pass	Pass	Pass
DENBIGH.	dep	6.30	8.25	9.53	11.33	10.45	2.15	3.50	4.30	4.55	7.30	8.38
Denbigh Jn		6.32	8.27	9.55	11.35	10.50	2.17	3.52	4.35	4.57	7.33	8.40
Trefnant	arr	6.37	8.31	10.00	11.39	10X55	2.23	3.57	4.42	5.02	7.39	8.46
	dep	6.38	8.32	10.01	11.40	11X27	2.28	3.58	C	5.03	7.40	8.48
Llanerch Sdg									MO			
St.Asaph	arr	6.44	8.37	10.07	11.45	11.37	2.34	4.04		5.10	7.46	8.54
	dep	6.45	8.38	10.08	11.46	12.15	2.35	4.05		5.12	7.48	8.56
Rhuddlan	arr	6.51	8.43	10.14	11.51	12.25	2.41	4.11		5.19	7.55	9.03
	dep	6.52	8.43	10.15	11.52	12.35	2.42	4.12		5.22	7.56	9.04
Foryd Jn	arr	-	-	10.20	-	12.45	-	-		-	-	-
	dep	6.57	8.48	10.21	11.57	1.40	2.47	4.18		5.27	8.01	9.09
RHYL	arr	7.00	8.51	10.23	12.00	1.45	2.50	4.20		5.30	8.05	9.12

NOTES:

C   = Conditional Train **Denbigh Tickets of all Down Trains**
MO = Mondays Only   **collected at Trefnant.**
"X" in times indicate trains cross. @ Conditional stop.

Additional notes state:
"No.2. to make a trip to Foryd Pier when required".
"No.17 to work Foryd Pier Line when required"
"No.17 to shunt at St.Asaph for no.16".
"Engines of Nos. 13, 17 & 19 to perform shunting at Rhyl when required."

It will be seen from the above that most workings were Denbigh turns, the exceptions being the 6.50am Goods which was worked by Rhyl men, as was the 8.05pm passenger to Denbigh, returning from there at 8.38pm.

The public time table for December 1904 shows eight trains each way, departing Rhyl at 7.50am, 9.10am, 11.00am, 1.20pm, 3.00pm, 6.15pm, 7.35pm and 10.25pm, whilst departures from Denbigh were at 6.30am, 8.25am, 9.45am, 11.45am, 2.06pm, 3.00pm, 5.00pm and 8.13pm. From the personal recollections of the late Percy Harrison, who worked at Rhyl shed for most of his life, most of the passenger traffic along the branch before World War I was worked by Denbigh men, although Rhyl men worked the daily goods.

The public time table for May 1st to July 11th **1913** showed the usual increase in train services for the summer season, although holiday traffic did not penetrate significantly into the Vale of Clwyd at this time. Departures from Denbigh for this period were at 6.25am, 7.55am, 9.45am, 11.40am, 2.08pm, 3.26pm, 3.45pm, 5.03pm, 7.17pm, 7.55pm and 8.57pm, with departures from Rhyl at 7.40am, 8.30am, 9.10am, 10.55am, 1.17pm, 3.00pm, 4.23pm, 5.28pm, 6.25pm, 7.40pm and 10.55pm. Chester men in No.4 Link, working with a "DX" 0-6-0 tender locomotive worked the 4.37pm local along the coast to Rhyl, arriving at the Down Loop platform at 5.44pm. Once passengers had been discharged from the train, it drew forward and set back into the bay. It then worked the 6.25pm to Denbigh, due at 6.51pm. The stock was then shunted clear of the platform and the engine then went on shed for loco duties and to turn. A Denbigh loco and set of men with the Chester guard and coaches worked the 8.15pm to Ruthin, returning with the 8.37pm from Ruthin to Chester. At Denbigh, the local engine and men came off the stock, replaced by the Chester engine and men who departed for Mold and home at 9.08pm.

The outbreak of war in 1914 saw no variation to passenger traffic patterns along the Vale of Clwyd., only to the timings of certain trains, the April 1st to July 10th **1915** public time table listing eleven departures each way, daily.

There was a build-up of military traffic due to the establishment of Army Training Camps in the area, some of which made use of the Vale of Clwyd line, but because the traffic requirements were arranged at short notice, and did not follow a predicable pattern, were not listed in the timetables, probably appearing in the Special Traffic Notices.

It was the establishment of the Kinmel Park Military Railway that affected traffic on the Vale of Clwyd line, although this concerned the northern end of the line at Foryd Junction, and at the end of the war and into 1919. There was considerable traffic from Rhyl station to the camp, and this can be seen in the Working Time Table extract for the period commencing July 1st **1919**, reproduced in full elsewhere. It will be noted that there was a reduction in the number of ordinary passenger service trains working between Denbigh and Rhyl, to eight Up and nine Down trains, with one goods train each way. Of particular interest however, is the extent of the Military traffic from and to Kinmel Park Camp. Trains were worked by the Military Authorities to Rhyl, with an LNWR Pilotman in charge from Foryd Junction into Rhyl station. Footplate staff on these trains were provided by the Railway Operating Division of the Royal Engineers, using their own locomotives and stock. Trains were frequently very lengthy, and it must have been an extra-ordinary sight to see a passenger working weaving its way across the flat land between the coast and the camp. It will be noted that trains were admitted to the single line almost as soon as the preceding one had cleared the section. This may also have inhibited the passenger workings to Denbigh. Due to the Mutiny in March of that year, the camp was cleared of Canadian personnel, and was subsequently used for housing Welsh troops returning from France, for demobilisation, and whose stay would doubtless be of short duration. Driver

St.Asaph. 30th August 1961. BR Standard Class 4MT 4-6-0 No.**75020** draws away from St.Asaph station and is seen crossing over the river Elwy, north of the station on the final leg of the circuit, heading towards Foryd Junction and Rhyl, with one of the two Land Cruise workings in the final week of operation. The six coach formation was supplemented on alternate days with the Devon Belle observation coach. Although the loco headboard is missing, a coach roof-board can be seen on the second coach. Rhyl traincrew worked the majority of the Land Cruise trains from inception to the end, and the work supplemented the more routine work along the North Wales coast and over Vale of Clwyd line to Denbigh and Ruthin, although most of the work from Denbigh worked through Mold to Chester.   *Author's collection.*

Percy Harrison recalled that as a passed fireman, he spent most of those days acting as pilotman, and although he was supposed to get off the footplate once the Military train had cleared the LNWR track, frequently he remained on the footplate to and from the camp. Frequently the Military driver would 'persuade' Percy to cover for him whilst he disappeared in the town for the evening, rewarding his efforts with a packet of cigarettes on the last trip. Military Police were supposed to check the footplate every trip at Foryd Junction to ensure that no illicit travelling took place, but despite the mutiny and its attendant publicity, supervision was lax, and no-one bothered to look at the engine. It was not unknown for both fireman and driver to disappear for a while, although supervision of the trains on the LNWR main line between Foryd Junction and Rhyl meant that there had to be at least two persons visible on the footplate. It will be noted that for the first time, a Sunday service operated on this short part of the Vale of Clwyd line, albeit to the camp. It is understood that military trains working between the camp and Rhyl used the Denbigh bay platform, although through specials to and from other destinations used the main platform faces. It is believed that only two issues of the LNWR working time tables contained timing details of these trains.

After the camp was cleared of personnel, the line was operated by the LNWR on an "as required" basis, with occasional trips to the camp to collect stores being moved to other camps. A new line was built from the camp to the Quarry near St.George's, and although the LMS delivered empty and collected loaded wagons to and from the former army camp site, worked forward to the quarry by the Quarry Company, eventually the line as far as Foryd Junction was taken over by the Limestone Quarry Company, who worked their trains to the Foryd Pier line, with the LMS collecting and delivering from and to this point. This practice continued until the quarry, faced with heavy repairs to the track, replaced the line with lorries. The LNWR Working Time Table for July 11th **1921** still listed Kinmel Park Camp within the Vale of Clwyd timing pages, but no trains to the camp were listed. The Vale of Clwyd showed ten passenger trains between Denbigh and Rhyl, and eleven in the opposite direction, together with the daily goods, the daily trip from Rhyl to Foryd Pier, and a Mondays Only unbalanced trip from Denbigh to Rhyl. The 7.25am from Rhyl to Denbigh and the 7.16pm from Denbigh to Rhyl were designated "Motor" trains. This was a Rhyl based pull & push unit that worked the 8.10am and three other trips between Denbigh to Mold and return, and made its way back home with the 7.16pm to Rhyl. It is believed that Denbigh men worked the Mold service, although Rhyl men also signed for the route.

The LMS Working Time Table for July 9th to September 30th **1923** was of the same format as the LNWR issues, containing passenger and goods trains in chronological sequence in the one book, but showed little change to the train services, although as previously mentioned, the three lines to Denbigh now appeared in the same timetable, and the Kinmel Park Camp line had disappeared. There were eleven trains each way, with a variation on Thursdays and Saturdays when an early evening trip was replaced by one two hours later. The daily freight to Foryd Pier had been reduced to Mondays, Wednesdays and Fridays only, and the Motor Train worked through to Chester on its second run, returning from there at 11.55am due Denbigh at 1.15pm. It then made two return trips to Mold before working back to Rhyl. It worked another trip to Denbigh and back

on Thursdays, the equivalent Saturdays Only trip in the care of a conventional locomotive and stock working. The daily goods worked from and to Rhyl, running later on Mondays, to cater for Market traffic.

During the General Strike the service was reduced to four passenger trips each way, at 7.25am, 9.19am, 2.43pm and 5.53pm from Denbigh, returning at 7.53am, 11.00am, 5.50pm and 7.30pm from Rhyl. Presumably the freight train still made its daily journey. By September, the Winter Time Tables showed twelve trains between Denbigh and Rhyl Mondays to Fridays (13 on Thursdays and Saturdays), and thirteen in the opposite direction (fifteen on Thursdays and sixteen on Saturdays). The freight time table for the period showed the daily goods to and from Denbigh running in approximately the same times, whilst the thrice weekly trip to Foryd Pier had changed to Tuesdays, Thursdays and Saturdays. A new working departed Denbigh at 5.10am from Denbigh to Mold Junction via Foryd Junction.

By **1934** passenger traffic had increased and there were sixteen trains daily between Denbigh and Rhyl (seventeen on Thursdays and Saturdays) and seventeen between Rhyl and Denbigh ((eighteen on Thursdays, nineteen on Saturdays). The 4.25pm and 7.10pm from Rhyl worked daily through to Corwen from Rhyl, as did the 9.25pm on Wednesdays and Saturdays Only. By this time the daily early morning freight to Mold Junction had been withdrawn, but the Foryd Pier trip had reverted to a daily service. The single daily freight trip between Rhyl and Denbigh and return continued as before.

The summer of **1939** saw the traffic along the line at its peak. nineteen trains worked between Denbigh and Rhyl on weekdays, (twenty on Thursdays, and twenty one on Saturdays) and ten on Sundays, with eighteen between Rhyl and Denbigh weekdays, (nineteen on Thursdays and twenty one on Saturdays) and ten on Sundays. The freight service remained unchanged.

A regular feature on all LMS lines was the working of Tariff vans, usually dedicated vehicles attached to passenger workings which nevertheless followed a controlled schedule. These worked from Chester, Liverpool Park Lane, Broad Street, Camden and Rhyl, and traversed the Vale of Clwyd on the 6.00am or the 1.15pm from Rhyl and in the reverse direction on the 1.50pm Denbigh to Rhyl. Vans involved in the *List of Tariff Vans* dated 1934 were as follows:

6.00am Rhyl to Denbigh included Vans 149 (from Chester); 302 (from Liverpool); 435 and 436 (from Rhyl).
1.15pm Rhyl to Denbigh included Van 322

Whilst there was a reasonable volume of Newspaper and Parcels traffic along the branch, there was insufficient to justify a dedicated van to the line. Space was provided on certain workings, according to the booklet *"Instructions for Dealing With Parcels Traffic"* published by the LMS, the copy to hand dated November 1938, the principal feeder train being the 2.05am Parcels train from Crewe to Holyhead, which included vans off the 1.25am from Manchester Exchange to Chester. Traffic for the branch was transferred at Rhyl. Other workings that carried Parcels or News Traffic were the 2.45am (MX) Crewe to Bangor, 3.15am (SuO) Crewe to Bangor. Traffic from the branch was generally worked to Rhyl and thence forward by ordinary service trains.

The Emergency Time Tables, brought out on 11th September 1939 showed the passenger service reduced to six trains from Denbigh to

Rhyl and seven in the opposite direction, with the 4.25pm and 7.10pm working through to Corwen. By October 1940 this had increased to ten trains from Denbigh and ten from Rhyl (twelve on Saturdays). Freight remained unchanged. There were no Sunday services.

By October **1944** the passenger service had been reduced to nine trains each way between Denbigh and Rhyl, weekdays, (ten on Saturdays). Again, no change to the freight train frequency.

The summer of **1948** saw the services over the line at ten each way between Denbigh and Rhyl on weekdays and eleven on Thursdays and Saturdays. This had increased to eleven trains (thirteen on Thursdays and Saturdays) between Denbigh to Rhyl and Ten between Rhyl and Denbigh (eleven on Thursdays, twelve on Saturdays and ten between Rhyl and Denbigh weekdays, and twelve on Saturdays. Again, no change to the freight services.

The final summer of passenger services on the line saw the service much reduced, five trains each way between Denbigh and Rhyl on weekdays and eight on Saturdays. Apart from variations in timings, the freight service remained unchanged throughout.

From September **1955**, following closure of Denbigh shed, traffic over the line was significantly reduced, the Working Time Tables showing a Class C Parcels Train leaving Rhyl at 5.20am, arriving Denbigh at 5.43am; the 7.40am Class K freight to Denbigh calling at Rhuddlan (11 minutes), St.Asaph (50 minutes) and Trefnant (10 minutes) due Denbigh at 9.30am; a Light Engine off Rhyl Shed at 4.20pm to work the 5.00pm passenger to Ruthin. In the reverse direction, the Class K freight worked back to Rhyl, departing Denbigh at 11.30am, calling at Trefnant (15 minutes), St.Asaph (30 minutes) and Rhuddlan (21 minutes) arriving at Rhyl yard at 2.20pm. Other movements to Rhyl were two light engines weekdays (one on Saturdays) to the shed at 6.05pm, another, daily, at 9.00pm after working the 8.25pm from Ruthin, and a third at 10.05pm (SX) after working the 8.35pm from Chester. This working was extended to Ruthin on Saturdays, and after working the 10.30pm from Ruthin to Denbigh, departed at 10.53pm L.E. to Rhyl shed.

The line was used on several occasions for excursion traffic from various towns in North Wales, and on more than one occasion, Sunday School specials were worked from Rhos, Wrexham, and Mold to Rhyl, travelling via the Wrexham, Mold and Connah's Quay line between Wrexham and Hope High level, often picking up at intermediate stations, and thence via the spur to the Mold and Denbigh line. At Denbigh the locomotive would run round its train for the final leg to Rhyl. In the early 1950's, Day and Half Day Excursions would be run on summer Saturdays, picking up on the route, and all were well patronised. Services were timed to arrive at Rhyl before mid-day, and often started the return journey after the traffic on the main line had subsided. Other excursions were run from the Western Region, again run as Sunday School excursions. Dolgellau, on the Ruabon to Barmouth line was a popular starting point. Of particular interest was the fact that Western Region,(GWR design) locomotives were used throughout, usually Collett 0-6-0's, but on one memorable occasion, 'Dukedog' 4-4-0 No.**9024** piloting a Collett 0-6-0 worked into Rhyl. Gwyn Parry photographed the special pulling out of the Down Loop platform on the return journey. It was all the more interesting in that this locomotive, with its outside cranks, was supposed to be prohibited from working over the DR&C and the VofC lines.

With the removal of the passenger services, there was no need to retain the intermediate block sections between Foryd Junction and Denbigh, and consequently these were taken out of use, replacing a single section. This apart, traffic over the line during the winter period remained constant. The summer period saw increased activity with the passage of the Land Cruise trains.

The final chapter in the Vale of Clwyd line was with the withdrawal of all services between Ruthin and Corwen, on the Denbigh, Ruthin & Corwen line, and between Denbigh and Rhydymwyn on the Chester line. The only access to Denbigh was over the Vale of Clwyd line. The Freight Working Time Table (Section G) for the period 9th September 1963 to 14th June 1964 showed an early morning mail train departing Rhyl daily at 5.15am to Ruthin (Reporting Number 8D92) arriving Denbigh 5.40am dep. 5.50am arr Ruthin at 6.10am, booked to call at Ruthin Lime Sidings if required.. It returned to Denbigh at 7.00am and after shunting worked back to Rhyl at 9.30am, Reporting Number 9D37, booked at St.Asaph from 9.45am until 10.05am, and at Rhuddlan from 10.15am until 10.25am. It was booked to pass Foryd Junction at 10.38am and arrived at Rhyl yard at 10.43am. The second working was a Saturdays Excepted working, departing Rhyl at 11.25am Reporting Number 9D85 and worked non stop to Denbigh, due 11.55am. Once it had cleared the long section from Foryd Junction, another working departed from Rhyl at 12.05pm (SX) (Reporting Number 9D88) to Kinmel Sidings, due 12.15pm. After thirty minutes it returned as 9D07 to Rhyl Yard. Meanwhile the locomotive standing in Denbigh yard worked forward at 1.10pm to Ruthin as the 9D39 due 1.30pm where it shunted as required until 2.10pm when it worked back to Denbigh as 9D39. After a further bout of shunting at Denbigh it worked back to Ruthin at 3.30pm as 9D85 due 3.50pm where it shunted as required until 4.25pm when it returned as 9D35 to Denbigh. due 4.45pm. After a further bout of shunting it departed to Rhyl at 6.10pm as 6D11 passing Foryd Junction at 6.30pm and arrived Rhyl at 6.36pm. A variation of this arrangement was operated during the summer of 1964, the alteration being the withdrawal of the second trip working from Denbigh to Ruthin, the loco now remaining at Ruthin until 3.30pm. It returned to Rhyl at 5.45pm. These timings remained in force until the commencement of services on 14th June 1965, when all reference to the workings was taken out of the Freight Working Time Tables, and was included in the local Trip and Shunting Engine Notices.

The North Wales Egg Train.

In 1913 The Railway Gazette reported in its 21st February issue, that the National Poultry Organisation Society had decided to run a demonstration train over the London & North Western and Cambrian Railways in North Wales in April and May, in conjunction with The Agricultural Organisation Society. The tour was provisionally scheduled to visit 30 centres in the counties of Flint, Denbigh, Carnarvon, Anglesea (sic), Merioneth and Montgomery.

The issue of 28th March announced that the dates for the visit had been agreed from April 23rd to May 6th. The first call was to be at Mold, after which various points in the Clwyd Valley were visited, after which the train returned to the coast via Denbigh, and proceeded to the Vale of Conway and Anglesey. The train then proceeded to Carnarvon and thence to Pwllheli. It was announced that the London & North Western Railway had placed at the disposal of the societies two of its largest vans. One was fitted with electric light, and a portion was made into a dark room, wherein the testing

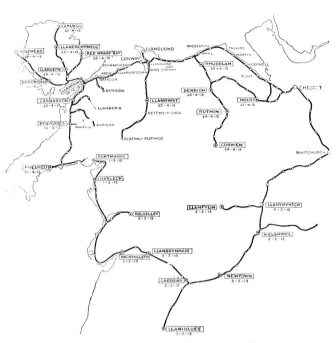

Itinerary of Egg and Poultry Demonstration.

eggs could be determined by examining the egg over a strong light, which could then be graded accordingly, or rejected if seen to be flawed. Current Dutch practice was also demonstrated by Mr Edward Brown, F.L.S. which he had secured on a recent visit to that country. The report concluded that the train was also equipped with numerous models, appliances, charts, diagrams and photographs. The train was accompanied by representatives of the Board of Agriculture, the Welsh County Councils and the County Education Committees, and the demonstration was enthusiastically supported. The final report on the train was published in the issue dated 13th June, which informed readers that the current issue of *Illustrated Poultry Record* contained an article on the tour by Mr B.W. Finberg, who had been responsible for the arrangements. The report pointed out that with one or two exceptions, the 27 places where the train had stopped were comparatively small towns or villages, where station accommodation was limited, and several problems had to be overcome before the vehicles could be placed in positions easily accessible to the public. Lectures and demonstrations took up to several hours at each place and where it was not possible to allow the train to remain in the station platforms, the stock was positioned in adjacent sidings, and portable steps provided. There was a large staff of lecturers and demonstrators which necessitated adequate provision of sufficient eatables and drinkables in a 65ft restaurant car, which was part of the train formation. The report commented that vehicles of this length were seldom if ever operated on some of the lines traversed, which called for very careful shunting. It appeared that prior to the visit of the train, a vehicle of the same length as the coach was sent to the various stations and sidings in order to ascertain that the scheduled arrangements were practical and could be undertaken in complete safety. The restaurant car was provisioned from Euston, an attendant travelled down daily with the necessary supplies, while a Chef and two attendants prepared and served meals. Nothing was left to chance, and prior to commencing the tour, various members of the societies organising the trip made several journeys to the London carriage sheds to explain exactly what was required to convert the vans into an egg-testing room. The whole train was worked as a special over the L&NW and Cambrian railways and a four page notice was issued to the staff for the purpose, which gave the daily scheduled times.

of eggs was demonstrated.

The issue dated May 16th gave details of the tour, and produced the map illustrated here. The train started from Euston on April 23rd, and had covered 400miles by the time it returned on May 6th. Arrangements were made jointly by the L&NW and Cambrian Railways and were satisfactorily carried out at every stage of the journey and both Welsh and English literature was freely distributed. The make-up of the train consisted of the aforementioned two large vans, and a restaurant car for the staff of the L&NWR. The dark room provided facilities to demonstrate scientific investigations, and proved to the audiences, how the grades and characteristic of the

Foryd Junction. 29th October 1957. Access to the Vale of Clwyd line was at Foryd Junction, controlled from a signal box of the same name, which was located on the Down side. The Chester and Holyhead main line was four track at this point, which meant that traffic off the branch had to cross the Down Slow and Fast Lines, connecting with the Up Fast, seen here. It was usual for Up trains off the branch to cross over to the Up slow via the facing crossover shown in the foreground. The lines crossed over a minor path on bridge 78A, seen here. In the centre foreground a gantry with three arms protects the crossing and just visible beyond the gantry the line crosses over the Foryd Pier line. In the haze, a freight train can be seen receding in the distance on the Down Slow line. A lookout is standing level with the box between the Down and Up lines, whilst a bowler hatted official strides purposefully towards the signal box. Notice the two arm bracket signal on the branch, the taller of the signal posts specifying the Up Fast main line.
British Railways London Midland Region.

THE LAND CRUISE TRAINS

During 1951, *The Festival Land Cruise* trains were introduced over the route, from Mondays to Fridays during the peak holiday season, starting from Rhyl to Denbigh and Corwen, where they joined Western Region metals, then worked through Dolgellau to Barmouth, where a break for refreshments was made. The working then continued along the Cambrian Coast to Afonwen, where the train regained LM tracks, and worked through Caernarfon and Bangor back to Rhyl. These trains were so popular that the following year a second train was introduced starting at Llandudno, which made its way down the coast to Rhyl where it reversed and followed the first train around the circuit. Motive power in the first few years was provided by Rhyl shed, using Ivatt Class 2 2-6-0 tender engines, which proved ideal for the six coach trains. Timings were adjusted from 1952 so that the Rhyl train departed at 9.56am, running under Reporting Number W662. Water was taken at Corwen, and Barmouth was reached at 12.46pm. Departure was at 2.25pm and a stop for water was made at Caernarfon at 4.23pm. The arrival at Rhyl was at 5.35pm. Meanwhile the Llandudno train was combined with the 9.56am to Crewe as far as Rhyl, Reporting Number W663 where the Cruise stock was detached and worked onto the Down side by the station shunt locomotive to the Down Loop platform where the Class 2 engine attached, departing at 11.00am and arrived at Barmouth at 1.55pm. It resumed the circuit at 3.20pm heading along the coast for Afonwen at a leisurely 25 mph. Water was taken at Caernarfon at 5.21pm following which the train proceeded to Llandudno Junction running into the Up Side bay platform The stock was worked to Llandudno by a Bangor 2-6-4T which then returned it to the Junction for servicing. The 2-6-0 meanwhile set back out of the bay and worked L.E. to Rhyl. A radio commentary was provided in each car and the workings were described as the "Radio Land Cruise" trains.

During the summer period of 1953, the Land Cruise trains ran as before, appropriately named *The Coronation Land Cruise*. Timings and stock for both trains were the same as in 1952. The summer of

1954 saw the Land Cruise trains continue to increase in popularity, and new trains were introduced to cater for the demand. On Tuesdays and Thursdays, a working started from Pwllheli departing at 10.10am (Reporting Number W667), which worked along the coast to Barmouth, where it took water, then across the Mawddach estuary where it turned east and headed inland as far as Corwen to join LM Region metals, before proceeding up the Vale of Clwyd to Rhyl, where a long break was taken, before resuming its circular path along the coast to Caernarfon and then to Afonwen, where it reversed and headed for Pwllheli. The work was undertaken by Pwllheli men working ex GWR Collett 0-6-0 tender engines, which provided an interesting distraction in the heartland of the LNWR. LM Pilotmen joined the train at Corwen and Rhyl. Alas the 'foreign' locomotive invasion only lasted a few days, until standard BR engines could be transferred to cover the work. A fourth train started at Llandudno Junction, (Reporting Number W669) and proceeded to Caernarfon, following the Pwllheli train from Afonwen to Barmouth, with the long break taken at Barmouth. This train was run on Tuesdays, Wednesdays and Thursdays, and subsequently ran Mondays to Fridays the following year. It returned along the coast as far as Caernarfon, where the loco ran round the stock before returning to Llandudno Junction.

The summer of 1956 saw a variation to the pattern of Land Cruise trains, in that The Rhyl train worked the circuit as formerly, whilst the Llandudno Land Cruise now reversed at Barmouth Junction and headed south to Aberdovey, due 1.50pm. It departed there at 3.30pm and worked up the coast to Afonwen, thence to Caernarfon and back to Llandudno. The Pwllheli Land Cruise worked as previously, departing at 10.10am, and the Section "L" and "J" Western Region Working Time Tables shows the train's path as far as Corwen, but fails to show up in the LM Region time table! Nevertheless the timings were subsequently printed in the appropriate weekly Special Traffic Notices. The Cruise starting at Llandudno Junction and working to Caernarfon and thence up the Cambrian Coast to

Rhyl. August 1958. An innovation for the Land Cruise workings in 1958 was the introduction of the **Land Cruise Lounge** carriage which was formerly the **Devon Belle** Observation Coach. The bar was a very popular attraction, and well patronised. There was, however, the need to turn the coach after each working. The relevant Land Cruise drew into Platform 1 - the main Up platform. The yard shunter came off the shed and after attaching to the observation coach, and detaching from the rest of the stock, set back into the shed yard, ran round the coach and propelled it onto the locomotive turntable, which was 60ft in diameter, and could just accommodate the vehicle. After turning, it was drawn through the station and propelled into the sidings on the Down side, where it was reunited with the stock for the following day's working before being placed into the carriage shed for cleaning and servicing. Occasionally, however, the turntable was out of use, and it then became necessary to work the coach to Llandudno Junction, for turning there. This was the situation on this occasion, and the yard shunter, Rhyl's resident Class 3F 0-6-0T No.**47350** is seen here attaching it to the rear of a Down working. Once turned at the Junction, it would be worked back to Rhyl and attached to the stock. *Huw Edwards*

Barmouth does not appear to figure in any publication, and it must be presumed that this was an early casualty. The omission in the LM Region Western Division Working Time Table is repeated the following year,

During 1958, the Pullman Observation Coach that formerly worked on *The Devon Belle* was transferred to the London Midland Region for inclusion in the Land Cruise formation, for which it was especially repainted. The Pullman Car Crest was replaced by the B.R. Emblem, and the coach carried the inscription *The Land Cruise Lounge* along each side of the coach. Huw Edwards took a picture of the coach being detached from the train at Rhyl station, prior to turning in readiness for the next day's working.

In the summer of 1959 there was a revision of the Land Cruise services. A new train left Rhyl at 9.25 for Cricieth, via Caernarfon, where it stopped for water, and then climbed over Pant Glas summit before descending to the Cambrian Coast, passing through Afonwen at 11.44am. On the LMR its Reporting Number was 400, but once on Western Region metals it was became 1945! It arrived at Cricieth at 11.50, and 55 minutes were allowed for sight-seeing before the train moved on to Barmouth (10 minutes). After crossing over the Mawddach estuary, it headed inland through Dolgellau, following the path of the TThO Cruise from Pwllheli, (Reporting Number 1940) which was running a couple of hours in front. Water was taken by both trains at Corwen before gaining DR&C metals. At long last the LM Region included paths for both trains in the Working Time Table, the Pwllheli train arriving at Rhyl at 1.58pm, working forward to Barmouth via Caernarfon and Afonwen. The 9.25am Rhyl to Cricieth, Barmouth and Corwen train arrived back at its starting point at 4.27pm. However a casualty this year was the original Rhyl Land Cruise that commenced over the DR&C., working the circuit in a clockwise direction. The 9.48am Llandudno to Aberdovey train appeared in the local time table pages for the first time, departing Rhyl at 10.38am. The timings for the rest of the run were the same as previous years.

In the summer of 1960, there were modifications to the Land Cruises. The 9.48am from Llandudno to Aberdovey, returning via Caernarfon was named *The Cambrian Radio Land Cruise* and was given the Reporting Number 1V61 on the Western Region (the LM Region number was 412). The 10.10am Pwllheli to Barmouth, Corwen and Rhyl ran in the same times. The 9.25am Rhyl to Cricieth, Barmouth and Corwen to Rhyl was given the name *The Welsh Chieftain* and ran on WR metals as 1V63 whilst a new diesel train ran from Llandudno (dep 2.30pm) to Corwen, due there at 4.20pm, and returning after a 35 minute break. Its Reporting Number on the Western Region was 1V62 out, 1M56 return, and was called *The Clwyd Ranger*. It ran on Tuesdays and Wednesdays only.

In 1961, despite the fact that the Western Region Section ''J'' Working Time Tables no longer showed the Land Cruise workings, in fact the Pwllheli trains ran as usual on Tuesdays and Thursdays in the same timings, whilst a new working, 1V63, departing Rhyl at 9.15am worked to Towyn on the Cambrian Coast, via the North Wales coast to Caernarfon, then Afonwen and Barmouth to Towyn due 12.55pm. The loco was a Rhyl based 75xxx Class 4 4-6-0 worked throughout by volunteer Bangor men, frequently Wil Bach Bob Shunt. The stock was parked in Towyn yard for two and a half hours, whilst the loco was scheduled to return tender first to Morfa

Mawddach to turn on the triangle, returning tender first back to Towyn. There was barely time to attend to the loco duties before it was time to return to Rhyl. On the second day the locomen asked permission to detach, and run round the triangle to turn and re-couple, to make use of the standing time whilst waiting for the road at Morfa Mawddach on the outward leg, then work the train to Towyn tender first, which gave them ample time to clean the fire and have a break. Fortunately commonsense prevailed and this procedure was approved and working accordingly for the rest of the season. The return working Reporting Number was 1M59.

It s not known if *The Clwyd Ranger* operated during that summer, but a scheduled DMU scheduled from Llandudno to Rhyl ran in the same times.

So the Land Cruise trains passed out of existence. They were an integral part of the North Wales holiday scene throughout the fifties, and opened out the country to thousands of holidaymakers. Speed was kept deliberately slow so that the scenery could be viewed and savoured.

Rhyl. July 1952. For the first few years of Land Cruise train workings, Ivatt Class 2MT 2-6-0 locomotives were drafted in at the commencement of the season to work the trains, and subsequently some remained at the shed throughout the year. They were ideally suited for the job, were regarded with affection by all who worked on the trains. Here No.**46428** stands at No.1 Up platform after having completed the circuit. The battered Reporting Number Board on the top lamp iron gives no clue as to the number, but was in fact W662, whilst underneath it clipped on the smokebox door hand-rail, hangs the almost indistinguishable headboard proclaiming **North Wales Radio Land Cruise**. A few stragglers are making their way along the platform to the main entrance, and presumably back to the Hotels, Guest Houses and Boarding Houses for an evening meal. The station clock on platform 2 proclaims the time as 5.35pm, so arrival at the destination must have been a couple of minutes early. Once the stock is empty, the coaches will be drawn out of the platform road and worked to the Carriage Shed for cleaning.   *Gordon Coltas.*

64 Vale of Clwyd Branch (Single Line) and Kinmel Park Camp Military Railway (Single Line).

Train Staff Stations—Foryd Junction, Rhuddlan, St. Asaph, Trefnant, and Denbigh Junction.

Passenger Trains can cross each other only at Denbigh Junction, Trefnant, St. Asaph, and Foryd Junction.

Miles.	DOWN TRAINS. Week Days.	1	2	3	4	5	6	7	8	9	10	11	12	13
		Mails	Goods	Goods	Pass.	Pass.	Pass.	Goods	Pass.	Pass.	Pass.	Pass	Pass.	Pass.
								TThO						
		a.m.	a.m.	a.m.	a.m.	a.m.	a.m.	a.m.	a.m.	a.m.	p.m.	p.m.	p.m.	p.m.
...	RHYL ....dep.	5 40	5 50	6 25	7 28	8 10	8 55	10 10	11 0	11 18	1 25	2 15	4 10	4 35
1	Foryd Jct. .... arr.	5§43	5§55	6§30	7§31	8§15	8§58	10§14	11 §3	11§23	1§28	2§20	4§13	4§38
	,, ,, Pier Line ...dep.	...	6 5	...	...	8 22	...	10 20	...	11 30	...	2 27	...	4 47
...	Kinmel Park Camp arr.	...	6 25	...	...	8 33	...	...	...	11 41	...	2 38	...	4 58
3⅜	Rhuddlan .... arr.	5 48	...	6 50	7 36	...	9 3	...	11 8	...	1 33	...	4 18	...
	Rhuddlan dep.	5 49	...	7 25	7 37	...	9 4	...	11 9	...	1 34	...	4 20	...
5⅞	St. Asaph .... arr.	5 55	...	7 35	7 43	...	9 10	...	11 15	...	1 40	...	4 25	...
	St. Asaph dep.	5 57	..	8 20	7 46	...	9 12	...	11 17	...	1 42	...	4 29	...
7⅝	Llanerch Siding	...	...	X	...	...	...	...	...	...	...	...	...	...
8⅝	Trefnant................. arr.	6 2	...	8 30	7 51	...	9 17	...	11 22	...	1 47	...	4 34	...
	Trefnant dep.	6 3	...	9 5	7 54	...	9 20	...	11 25	...	1 53	...	4 38	...
10	Denbigh Junction	6 §7	...	9§11	7§58	...	9§24	...	11§29	...	1§57	...	4§42	...
11¼	DENBIGH.................. arr.	6 10	...	9 15	8 1	...	9 27	...	11 32	...	2 0	...	4 45	...

DOWN TRAINS. Week Days.	14	15	16	17	18	19	20	21	22	23	24	25	26	27
	Pass.	Pass	Pass.	Pass.	Pass.	Pass.	Pass	Pass	Pass.	Pass	SUNDAYS.	Pass	Pass	Pass
		SO				SO	S	SO	S	SO				
	p.m.	p.m.	p.m.	p.m.	p.m.	p.m.	p.m.	p.m.	p.m.	p.m.		p.m.	p.m.	p.m
RHYL.........................dep.	5 57	6 5	6 55	7 20	8 55	9 5	10 0	10 20	11 10	11 35		3 0	8 0	10 20
Foryd Jct. ....arr.	6 §0	6§10	6§58	7§25	8§58	9§10	10 §5	10§25	11§15	11§40		3 §5	8 §5	10§25
,, ,, Pier Line ...dep.	...	6 17	...	7 32	...	9 17	10 12	10 32	11 22	11 47		3 12	8 12	10 32
Kinmel Park Camp arr.		6 28	...	7 43	...	9 28	10 23	10 43	11 33	11 58		3 23	8 23	10 43
Rhuddlan .... arr.	6 5	...	7 3	...	9 3	...	...	...	...	...		...	...	...
Rhuddlan dep.	6 6	...	7 4	...	9 4	...	...	...	...	...		...	...	...
St. Asaph .... arr.	6 12	...	7 10	...	9 10	...	...	...	...	...		...	...	...
St. Asaph dep.	6 14	...	7 12	...	9 12	...	...	...	...	...		...	...	...
Llanerch Siding	...	...	...	...	...	...	...	...	...	...		...	...	...
Trefnant .... arr.	6 19	...	7 17	...	9 17	...	...	...	...	...		...	...	...
Trefnant dep.	6 23	...	7 20	...	9 20	...	...	...	...	...		...	...	...
Denbigh Junction..............	6§27	...	7§24	...	9§24	...	...	...	...	...		...	...	...
DENBIGH.................. arr.	6 30	...	7 27	...	9 27	...	...	...	...	...		...	...	...

UP TRAINS. Week Days.	28	29	30	31	32	33	34	35	36	37	38	39	40	41
	Goods	Pass	Pass.	Pass	Pass.	Goods	Pass.	Pass.	Pass		Pass.	Pass	Goods	1.0 p.m. from Ruthin.
	a.m.	a.m.	a.m.	a.m.	a.m.	a.m.	p.m.	p.m.	p.m.		p.m.	p.m.	p.m.	
DENBIGH.................dep.	...	...	7 25	...	9 24	TThO	12 3	...	1 45	...	2 55	...	3 30	
Denbigh Junction..............	...	...	7§28	...	9§27	...	12 §6	...	1§48	...	2§58	...	3§34	
Trefnant .... arr.	...	...	7 32	...	9 31	...	12 10	...	1 52	...	3 2	...	3 40	
Trefnant dep.	...	...	7 33	...	9 32	...	12 11	...	1 55	...	3 3	...	4 10	
Llanerch Siding	...	...	...	...	...	...	...	...	...	...	...	...	...	
St. Asaph .... arr.	...	...	7 38	...	9 37	...	12 16	...	2 0	...	3 8	...	4 20	
St. Asaph dep.	...	...	7 44	...	9 39	...	12 18	...	2 2	...	3 10	...	5 25	
Rhuddlan .... arr.	...	...	7 50	...	9 45	...	12 24	...	2 8	...	3 16	...	5 35	
Rhuddlan dep.	...	...	7 51	...	9 48	...	12 27	...	2 12	...	3 19	...	6 43	
Kinmel Park Camp dep.	4 20	7 22	...	9 15	...	...	...	1 35	...	...	...	3 20	...	
Foryd Jct. Pier Line ... arr.	4 40	7 33	...	9 26		10 40		1 46	...	...	...	3 31	...	
,, Junction...........dep.	4§55	7§40	7§56	9§33	9§53	10§50	12§32	1§53	2§17	...	3§24	3§40	6§50	
RHYL......................arr.	5 0	7 45	7 59	9 38	9 56	10 55	12†35	1 58	2 20	...	3 27	3 45	6 55	

UP TRAINS. Week Days.	42	43	44	45	46	47	48	49	50	51	52	53	54	55
	Pass.	Pass.	Pass	Pass.		Pass	Pass.	Pass.	Pass	Pass	SUNDAYS.	Pass	Pass	Pass
	p.m.	p.m.	p.m.	p.m.		p.m.	p.m.	p.m	p.m.	p.m.		p.m	p.m.	p.m
DENBIGH.................dep.	5 2	SO	...	5 55	...	...	8 2	SO	S	SO		...	...	...
Denbigh Junction..............	5§ 5	...	...	5§58	...	...	8 §5	...	...	...		...	...	...
Trefnant .... arr.	5 9	...	...	6 2	...	...	8 9	...	...	...		...	...	...
Trefnant dep.	5 10	...	...	6 3	...	...	8 10	...	...	...		...	...	...
Llanerch Siding	...	...	...	...	...	...	...	...	...	...		...	...	...
St. Asaph .... arr.	5 15	...	...	6 8	...	...	8 15	...	...	...		...	...	...
St. Asaph dep.	5 18	...	...	6 13	...	...	8 17	...	...	...		...	...	...
Rhuddlan .... arr.	5 24	...	...	6 19	...	...	8 23	...	...	...		...	...	...
Rhuddlan dep.	5 27	...	...	6 22	...	...	8 26	...	...	...		...	...	...
Kinmel Park Camp dep.	...	5 25	5 45	...	...	7 55	...	9 40	10 30	10 55		1 50	5 20	9 0
Foryd Jct. Pier Line ... arr.	...	5 36	5 56	...	...	8 6	...	9 51	10 41	11 6		2 1	5 31	9 11
,, Junction...........dep.	5§32	5§43	6 §3	6§27	...	8§13	8§31	9§58	10§48	11§13		2 §8	5§38	9§18
RHYL......................arr.	5 35	5 48	6 8	6 30	...	8 18	8 34	10 3	10 53	11 18		2 13	5 43	9 23

The Kinmel Park Camp Service is worked throughout by the Military Railway.

No. 34—†Public Bills 12.37 p.m.

Denbigh Tickets of all Down Trains to be collected at Trefnant.

Tickets of all Up Trains from Denbigh to be examined at Rhuddlan.

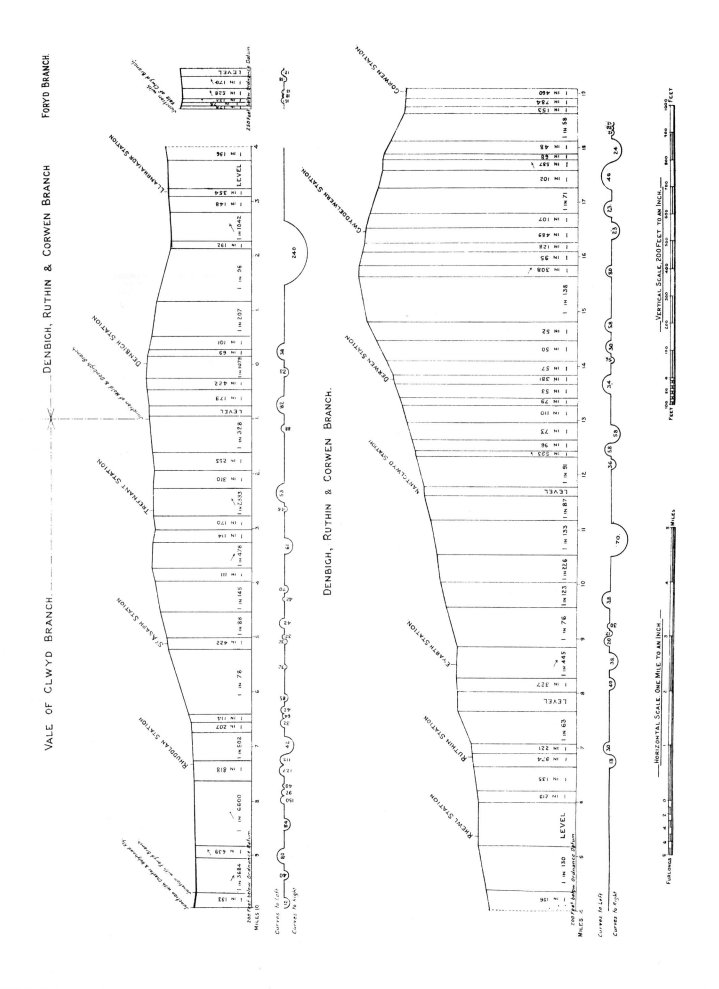

VALE OF CLWYD BRANCH.

DENBIGH, RUTHIN & CORWEN BRANCH

FORYD BRANCH.

DENBIGH, RUTHIN & CORWEN BRANCH.

VERTICAL SCALE, 200 FEET TO AN INCH

HORIZONTAL SCALE, ONE MILE TO AN INCH

Corwen. 7th August 1948. LMS Standard Class 2P 4-4-0 No.**675** stands at the Down platform after working the 5.12pm from Denbigh. This was a long term resident of Denbigh shed and the working was with Denbigh traincrew. Once the passengers had been cleared, the train drew forward into the Down side sidings in order to clear the platform for the 5.40pm Auto train from Ruabon due at 6.19pm. The Up platform could not be used as this was required for the 5.50pm from Bala which arrived at Corwen at 5.14pm. Once the section to Carrog had been cleared, the Western Region passenger departed for Wrexham at 6.20pm. Peace descended on the station once more, so the Denbigh men would draw forward and set back onto the Up side where they would detach the loco from its stock and proceed to the shed road on the Up side where they would turn, clean the fire, take water and pull coal forward on the loco. Once these duties were complete it would set back onto the stock, and draw them forward into the Up platform ready for departure time. The Western Region auto train would depart for Ruabon at 6.45pm, followed at 6.50pm by the LM train to Denbigh, where train crews were changed, the fresh crew then working engine and stock through to Chester. One or two unusual features about this former Great Western station. Notice the decorative valancing on the roof of the footbridge, the large nameboard with *Change for Denbigh and L.M.S. Railway* at the head of the ramp, duplicated at the opposite end of the platform. Notice too the small station signs suspended from the platform lamps.

W.A. Camwell

Corwen

The Great Western Railway owned the station at Corwen but under various Acts of Parliament, both companies had through booking rights. In 1925 the LMS paid a share of the administrative costs, including the a proportion of the wages of some staff. On the joint account were the Station Master (Class 2), a Goods Clerk Class 4, 2 Class 5 Clerks, 1 Junior Clerk, 2 Shunters Class 2, 4½ Signalmen Class 4, 1 Porter Signalman, 1 Checker, 1 Goods Porter, 1 Parcels Porter, 1 Porter Grade 1, 3 Porters Grade 2 and 1 Junior Numbertaker. The LMS Linesman attended to the single line token equipment and telephone circuits in Corwen East signal cabin

The LMS had a locomotive and operating staff based at Corwen, and shared (and paid) for the facilities in the locomotive yard, as well as for the use of the turntable, and water. When the GWR closed their locomotive depot, the facility was offered to the LMS, who found the terms unacceptable, and ceased stabling an engine overnight, although they continued to use all the other facilities. The men were

transferred to Denbigh

Most LMS trains made connections with the GWR, and although traffic over the latter was not very imaginative, through passenger bookings declined steadily from 1930 onwards and the withdrawal of services in 1953 came as no surprise. Apart from excursion traffic passing over the line, trains over the DR&C were local, and most terminated at Denbigh. Some worked through to Chester, but there is no evidence to show through coach workings outside these points. Two non corridor coaches generally sufficed.

LMS Country Lorry Services worked from Corwen, and were seen in the town on a regular basis. They also served the surrounding villages of Betws Gwerfyl Goch, Carrog, Cerrig-y-Druidion, Cynwyd, Glanrafon, Llandrillo and Maerdy, some in direct competition with the GWR who had stations in the village. The LMS lorries involved, however, were based at Ruthin and called on a daily basis.

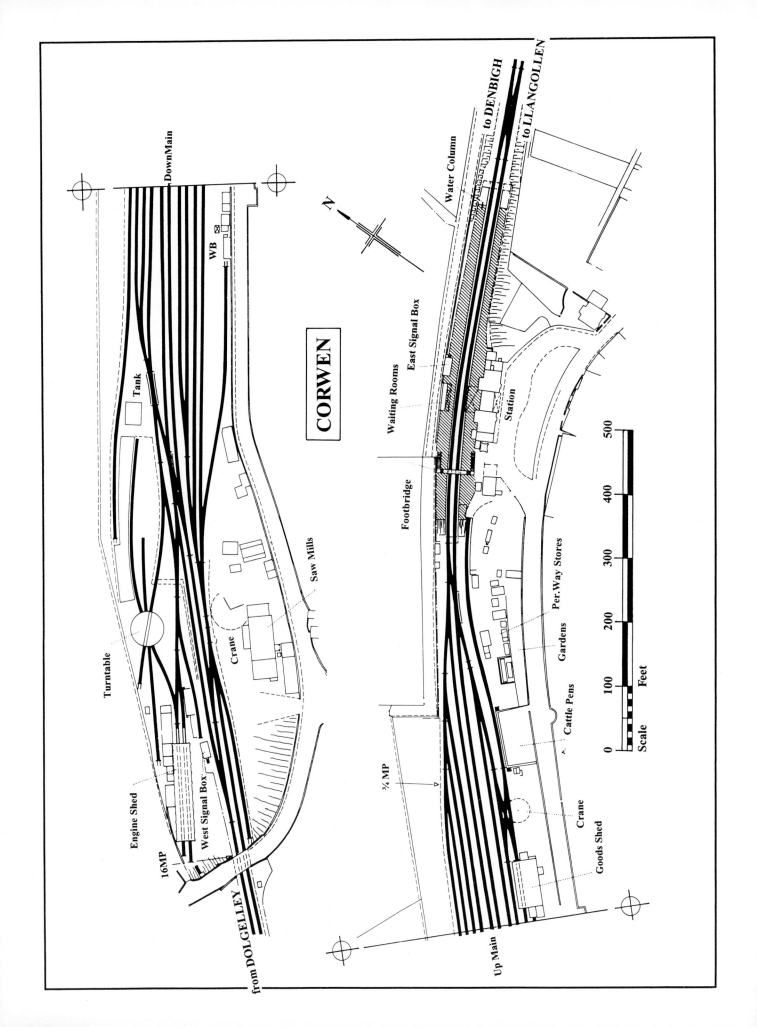

Corwen. 24th February 1961. Ex GWR Class 43xx 2-6-0 No.**6339**, a long term resident of Croes Newydd shed, pulls out of Corwen yard with a Down Class "H" freight. This was the 7.50am from Ruabon to Barmouth, worked by Croes Newydd men, who worked non stop to Corwen, apart from pausing at Llangollen (Goods) Junction signalbox awaiting the token. It was due Corwen at 8.47am and shunted the yard until departure at 10.27am and after stopping at Llandrillo for 12 minutes, worked through to Bala Town where Bala men relieved the Croes Newydd crew. Barmouth was reached at 2.24pm. The make-up of this train usually contained a high proportion of vans, as shown here. Interesting features to note are the single petrol tank wagon protected by the container flat trucks behind the tender, probably the continuous vacuum brake was connected to the tank wagon. Notice also the bogie bolster truck and the LMS brake van. Corwen West box is visible beyond the loco, and the water tower behind the last van. *Norman Jones.*

Corwen. 9th May 1949. LMS Standard Class 4P Compound 4-4-0 No.**40933** of Chester (6A) shed stands at the ramp of the Down platform after working the 10.25am from Chester. To find a Compound working to Corwen was unusual, but not rare, and it is likely that the Class 2P which normally worked this turn was unavailable. The Fireman, cigarette in mouth, pulls coal forward whilst his mate starts the injector to cool the boiler and stop the safety valves lifting, which was frowned upon by platform staff. Notice the style of lettering on the cabside, which was the old LMS numerals, and the former company's initials on the tender. This left hand drive loco was one of the penultimate batch of this design, new in 1927, and built by Vulcan Foundry. The stock would be drawn out of the platform and stored whilst the engine went on the loco siding for water and turning. It was not due to depart for Chester until 2.25pm so the crew would have time to rest and take things easy for a while. *E.S. Russell.*

Corwen. Friday, 24th February 1961. By this date London Midland engines and men were confined to one visit daily during the winter months, working the trip from Denbigh and return with the Class K freight. This was a leisurely working, the traincrew normally having the line to themselves, with plenty of time to pause at the remaining sidings to shunt. Latterly the loco used for this job was a BR Standard Class 2 2-6-0, in this case No.**78056** of Rhyl shed. In winter months, the limited protection afforded by the tender cab was welcome, particularly in bad weather, as one leg of the journey had to be worked tender first, on this occasion the return trip. The turn was normally worked by two drivers based at Denbigh, a remnant of the days when the town had its own locomotive department, the turns listed under Rhyl diagrams as "Denbigh Residential Men", although in truth, this only applied to the drivers. The fireman was drawn from Rhyl's complement, and that individual was required to travel to or from Rhyl by various means. *(top left)* Emrys Ingleby, as fireman, stands on top of the tender whilst the tank is topped up, whilst driver Norman Reed *(top right)* stands by the water valve awaiting the signal to turn off supplies. A slow response might lead to an involuntary bath. Note the 'fire devil' alongside the column, necessary in freezing weather to prevent icing up. *(lower),* shows both men observing the photographer. Although the 'bag' is still in the tender water filler, its flat shape suggests that the water supply has been turned off. The protection afforded by the tender cab can be seen, and whilst there is some protection, the cabs were usually draughty enough on all but the warmest of days, whilst working tender first.   *Norman Jones (3)*

Corwen. 24th May 1947. For many years the Corwen to Denbigh passenger services were largely in the hands of ex LNWR 5ft. 6ins. Class 1P 2-4-2T tank engines, with Rhyl and Denbigh sheds containing several members of the class. With the resumption of peacetime activities gathering pace, the arrears of maintenance was gradually being reduced, and the older engines were gradually being phased out. The days of the 2-4-2T's were numbered and before long, they had disappeared from these workings for ever. Their replacements were mainly Class 2P 4-4-0's, which were adequate for the workings, on two or three coach trains, interspersed by other types on odd occasions. Despite the workings using tank engines, it was the practice to turn them prior to working the return trip. LMS No.**6748**, on loan from Llandudno Junction shed to Denbigh, is seen here working the 3.45pm from Denbigh, with a set of three non corridor coaches. These little tanks were not the most comfortable of engines for working over the DR&C, the fireman having a somewhat poor deal in the cramped conditions. No one expressed deep regrets at their passing.   *W.A. Camwell.*

Corwen. 19th May 1961. Emrys Ingleby steadies the water bag and keeps a weather eye on the rising water level in the tender, whilst Driver Bill Jones waits for the signal to shut the valve. The loco was LMS Class 3F 0-6-0 No.**43618** and the working was the daily freight over the DR&C line in its last full year of operation. The weather conditions were not very favourable, the sky being grey and overcast, and a stiff wind made life unpleasant for tender first working. The duty was one of two turns worked by Denbigh Residential Men, sole survivors to remain based at Denbigh when that shed closed in September 1955. It will be seen that the footbridge cover has been removed, which caused discomfort for the passengers who needed to get to the Up platform. Despite the fact that the threat of closure was in the air, the station and its buildings are neat and tidy, although traffic had dwindled considerably.

Norman Jones.

Corwen. 1964. The Up side waiting shelter at Corwen was a small brick built structure, which could be surprisingly cosy on dark winter evenings, with a roaring fire of good loco coal supplying the heat. Once through the door, however, the small canopy gave little protection against the wind that swept through the station. In the summer months, it was pleasant to sit outside on one of the two types of benches on view. Beyond is Corwen East box, with the signalman on duty's bike propped against the brick base. Notice the spear fencing with the very dated poster imploring one to "Drinka Pinta wins the day". *G.H. Platt.*

Corwen. April 1965. Although the line from Barmouth to Corwen had only been closed a few months, the signal box had already assumed an air of dereliction. The paint had started to fade, the windows were no longer cleaned daily, grass was growing under the steps to the cabin and the frame room windows had been boarded over, a truly depressing sight. It remained in this condition for about a year, until the inevitable vandalism commenced, although perhaps it is a measure of progress to reflect that it survived intact as long as it did. Today the box would have been vandalised before the line closed. *W.G. Rear.*

Corwen. 5th November 1964. A more general view of the platforms and buildings at Corwen looking east towards Llangollen, in the final four weeks before the line closed. Despite the inevitability, there is still an air of cleanliness about the place, the signalman's bike is propped in its usual place, the track is weed free, and beyond the double canopy on the Down side a porter's barrow can be seen in the distance. *D. Thompson.*

Corwen. c.1923. The usual formation for passenger trains between Corwen and Denbigh was a 65 ton set of five six wheel stock in made-up sets nominally working the Llandudno District circuit in rotation. Motive power was one of the LNWR 2-4-2T, several examples of which were based at Denbigh, and subsequently out-stationed at Corwen. It was the practice to turn engines to face the direction of travel over this section of line, the LNWR paying the Great Western for the facility. Doubtless this was to ensure that the water level in the boiler covered the firebox crown whilst climbing to Gwyddelwern. On display are the usual array of vitreous enamel signs attached to walls and fences. Note also the ornamental lamps on each platform. The passengers under the canopy seem to be out-numbered by platform staff at the Dolgellau end of the Down platform.

D. Thompson.

Corwen. 1961. There were two signal boxes at Corwen. East box seen here was situated on the Up platform, and was a standard GWR design, housing a standard 34 lever frame. Two single line token instruments can be seen in the window, one each for the L.M. Region line to Denbigh and the other to Carrog. The signalman is seen walking in the six foot back to his box, carrying the wire hoop which contained the token. Regular passenger trains over the Denbigh, Ruthin & Corwen line had ceased in February 1953, although the Land Cruise and occasional excursion trains still used the line. The train standing at the Down platform was a regular working from Ruabon to Barmouth. Two passengers sit on the bench on the Up platform, awaiting a train towards Llangollen. Apart from the replacement of the attractive ornamental gas lamps by very austere electric ones, and the removal of the fence-mounted advertisement signs and the covering over the footbridge, very little else seems to have changed from the previous picture. *G.H. Platt.*

Corwen. 11th May 1949. LMS Standard Class 2P 4-4-0 No.**40646** wearing a 7D Rhyl shedplate and hauling two non corridor coaches, crosses from the L.M. Region single line to the Down platform at the east end of Corwen, with the 3.45pm from Denbigh, and worked by Denbigh men, due Corwen at 4.34pm. According to the Official transfer sheets, this locomotive had been transferred from Llandudno Junction four days previously, although it had formally been based at Denbigh (outstationed from Rhyl) until May 1948. These locomotives with their large driving wheels might have appeared unsuitable for the heavily graded line, but the lightweight train compensated for this. After the passengers had detrained, the stock was immediately drawn clear of the Down platform and set back on the Up side, after which the loco would go to the shed yard to turn, working back through to Rhyl departing at 5.00pm. The movement was necessary in order to clear the Down platform for the 3.45pm Wrexham to Bala auto train, due Corwen at 4.49pm and which worked forward at 4.55pm. There was a satisfactory exchange of passengers bound for stations on the D.R.& C. line off this connection. *E.S. Russell.*

Corwen. 9th May 1949. Auto trains were an integral part of the Western Region operating practice for their passenger services between Bala and Wrexham, perhaps reflecting the light loadings that existed on their trains. Here, 0-6-0PT No.**6404** draws into Corwen station with the 11.20pm from Ruabon to Bala, one trailer coach being sufficient for passenger needs. Although it is 1949, there are no visible signs of the change of ownership of the locomotive, and it is seen still sporting its number of the bufferbeam, and 'G.W.R.' on the tanks - a reluctance to admit to new political masters and one that survived longer on the Western Region than any other Region. This particular locomotive arrived at Croes Newydd from Birkenhead on 26th February 1949 although it 'floated' between Croes Newydd, Bala, Trawsfynydd and Penmaenpool sheds, until 4th December 1954 when it went for a holiday to Stafford Road. It returned to 84J eight weeks later and remained at the shed until 21st March 1959 when it moved to Oswestry. Its stay there was brief, and was withdrawn from service in June of the same year. *E.S. Russell.*

Corwen. 7th August 1948. Standard Class 2P 4-4-0 4-4-0 No.**675** of Denbigh shed negotiates the scissors crossover off the single line from Gwyddelwern onto the Down line east of the station, with the 5.12pm working from Denbigh, hauling the usual two coach non corridor set. Notice the Up line lower quadrant starting signals, whilst opposite on the Down side, a GWR token catcher with its receiving arm protruding through the rope netting, and the oil lamp on a wooden post strategically placed to illuminate the arm over which the firemen would loop the staff holder. L.M. Region trains used the Webb & Thompson design large staff for their section to Gwyddelwern, so could not use this facility, and the staff was handed over to the signalman at East box as the train drew up at the platform. The parallel lines climbed slightly towards Llangollen before the tracks diverged. The former Great Western line to Llangollen followed the course of the river Dee as it meanders along the valley floor whilst the L.M. Region line turned north and commenced climbing to the summit of the line beyond Gwyddelwern.

W.A. Camwell.

Corwen. 19th May 1961. Ex. Midland Railway Class 3F 0-6-0 No.**43618** working the daily Class K freight from Denbigh coasts down the gradient on the approach to Corwen. Beyond the three span bridge can be seen the Western Region line from Llangollen, the two lines meeting and running parallel for the final stretch into Corwen. This was the last full year of traffic working over the Denbigh, Ruthin & Corwen line, the line closing to all traffic eleven months later. By this time too, the turntable at Corwen had been taken out of use, and it was necessary for locomotives to work tender first one way. The lack of water supply between Ruthin and Corwen necessitated the use of tender engines on the job and a concession was made to the two Denbigh Residential drivers who worked the turn alternate weeks, who had the choice of working out of Denbigh tender or smokebox leading on the outward leg, the determining factor being the weather. On wet days, the trip could be depressing, although traincrews were philosophical about such things, and took it all in their stride. The Class 3 loco from Rhyl shed was a long term resident on the job, although latterly a BR Standard Class 2 2-6-0 complete with tender cab worked the job, which gave some measure of protection.

Corwen. May 1961. Fowler Class 3F 0-6-0 No.**43618** makes a vigorous attack on the climb out of Corwen with the daily return freight working to Denbigh, and seen here crossing the multi-span lattice girder bridge over the river Dee. The climb for the next few miles to the summit beyond Gwyddelwern was unrelenting, and firemen ensured they had a good head of steam on departure, in this instance, the safety valves are lifting, and making light work of this short Class K working. The photographer's location for this view was made known in advance, and both fireman and guard can be seen looking out for him. In the foreground in the centre of the river Dee can be seen a pillar which carried a footbridge over the river, but has long since been removed. *Norman Jones.*

Corwen. 1952. Class 2P 4-4-0 No.**40629**, nominally of Rhyl shed (6K), but usually outstationed at Denbigh, displaying the full 'BRITISH RAILWAYS' lettering on the tender hauls the usual load of two non corridor coaches over the six span lattice girder bridge across the River Dee on the climb towards Gwyddelwern with a through train for Denbigh and Chester via Mold. The weather must have been warm, for every drop light window in the carriage doors appear to be open. The loco is steaming well, and the fireman's control of smoke emission would satisfy even the sternest Locomotive Inspector. These four coupled locomotives were a common feature on passenger turns over this section of the line in its final years of operation.   *Author's collection.*

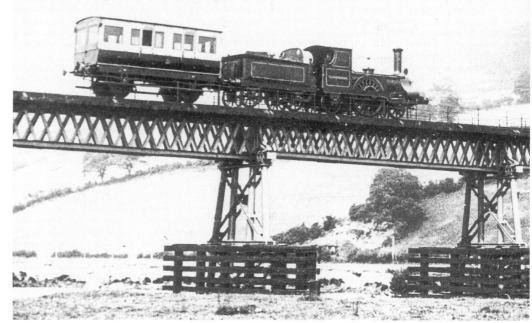

Corwen. c.1897. The six span lattice girder bridge over the River Dee at Corwen appeared to be a flimsy structure, but the section of line between Corwen East and Gwyddelwern was restricted only to locomotives above Class 5. In this view, we see the District Engineer's inspection train with the 'locomotive *'Engineer Bangor'* and four-wheel saloon. Notice the base of the support piers have not been concreted in.   *Author's collection.*

(right). **Gwyddelwern. 13th August 1953.** Although passenger services had ceased some six months earlier, very little had changed at the station. The building still sports its canopy over the short platform, the white platform edging reflecting the staff desire to maintain a tidy appearance for the passing Land Cruise trains that still traversed the line, and which were required to change single line staff tokens here. The Up Goods loop line looks to be still in regular use. The gradient eases beyond the platform for a short distance before resuming its climb at 1 in 128 to the summit of the line some three quarters of a mile away.   *The late H.C. Casserley.*

(left). **Gwyddelwern. 19th May 1961.** Porter signalman Andrew Jones hand the train staff for the forward section of line to Ruthin to fireman Emrys Ingleby, working the return daily freight to Denbigh. The Class 3F 0-6-0 locomotive was a regular performer on this duty. Note the small **"3"** on the cab side sheet, a relic of its Midland Railway days. These right hand drive engines were preferred to the more modern Class 4 equivalents, although the author has few affectionate memories about either design. *Norman Jones.*

Gwyddelwern

Captain Tyler approved the opening of the line from Ruthin to Gwyddelwern and the official opening date was set for 12th May 1863 but which was delayed, as mentioned elsewhere. Initially it was the temporary terminus of the line, until the extension to Corwen was completed, and at one time an engine shed existed here. Even today the village comprises only a few houses, but stone was quarried in the vicinity and eventually these were rail connected, providing valuable revenue for the line. The Dee Clwyd Granite Quarry had sidings connected in 1891 followed by the Craig Lelo quarry in 1924. Traffic from both of these quarries sustained the line until the late 1950's.

Gwyddelwern station was 2 miles 980 yards from Corwen and 9 miles 1104 yards from Derwen, (16¼ miles from Denbigh, 45½ miles from Chester) and consisted on a single platform on the Down side of the line with a goods loop on the Up. It was a crossing point on the single line, controlled by electric staff token system which persisted until the line closed. In common with other stations on the line, a canopy was fitted over the platform, but this was removed after regular train services ceased. A note in the Sectional Appendix to the Working Timetable dated March 1937 and again in the October 1960 edition states that any work to be done by a train must be performed inside the goods loop. It also states that at the Craig Lelo Quarry Company's siding, trains on arrival were to be placed on the loop, and whilst a train was working at the siding, no vehicles were to be on the main line unless attached to the engine. A brief examination of the gradient profile should explain this note!

DENBIGH RUTHIN AND CORWEN LINE.
GWYDDELWERN.

Williamson's Siding.
Dee Clwyd Granite Quarry.

1 Mile 17½ Chs. North of Gwyddelwern Station
132' 6"   15 M.P.

From Denbigh   To Corwen

49 Yards

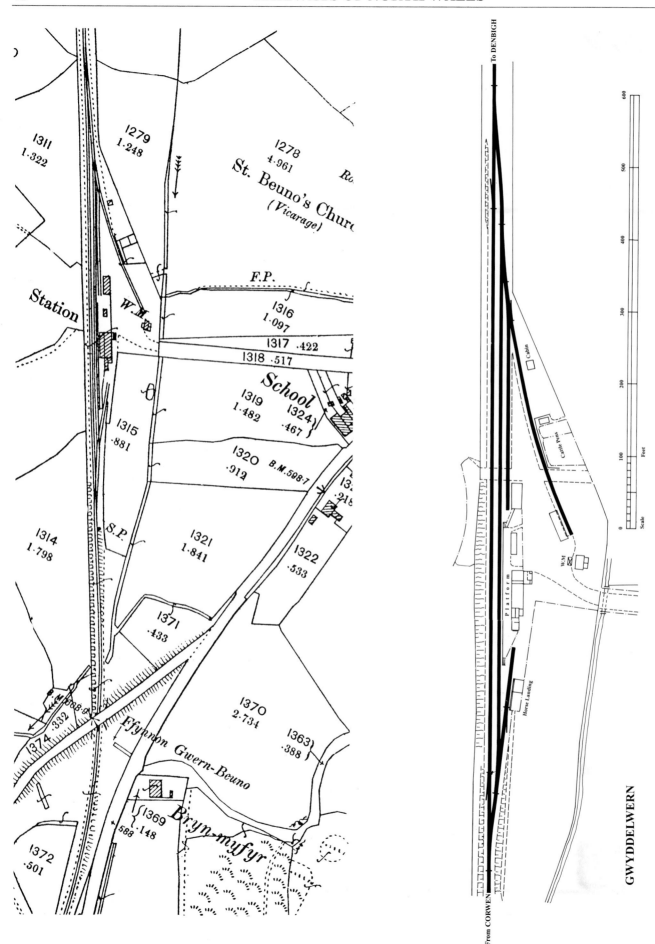

GWYDDELWERN

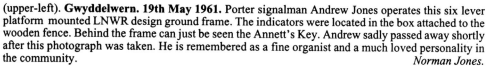

(upper-left). **Gwyddelwern. 19th May 1961.** Porter signalman Andrew Jones operates this six lever platform mounted LNWR design ground frame. The indicators were located in the box attached to the wooden fence. Behind the frame can just be seen the Annett's Key. Andrew sadly passed away shortly after this photograph was taken. He is remembered as a fine organist and a much loved personality in the community. *Norman Jones.*

(top-right). **Gwyddelwern. 1961.** At the Corwen end of the station stood one of the first concrete signal posts, produced by the LNWR about 1919, which served both Up and Down lines. The Up starter is lowered. At the foot of the post is a two lever ground frame, used to control the points to the Up Goods loop. This was interlocked from the station ground frame Annett's key by means of the rodding in the foreground. *G.H. Platt.*

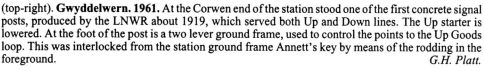

(lower). **Gwyddelwern. 19th May 1961.** Driver Bill Jones and Fireman Emrys Ingleby pose by the cab of Class 3F 0-6-0 No.**43618** on the outward trip to Corwen with the daily freight from Denbigh. The turntable at Corwen had been taken out of use and it was necessary to work tender first in one direction, which was a somewhat bleak prospect for train crews when the weather was inclement. It was, nevertheless, part of the job, and accepted without fuss. A far cry from the totally enclosed cab for the modern driver, although very few footplatemen today would freely return to the spartan conditions that were once the norm. *Norman Jones.*

(upper). **Gwyddelwern. Friday 24th February 1961.** BR Standard Class 2 2-6-0 No.**78056** stands at the platform with the daily return freight working from Corwen to Denbigh. The crew are doubtless in the station office, probably having a quiet chat and possibly a warm cup of tea. Progress was leisurely and any time lost could easily be made up without attracting the attention of the powers-that-be. Notice the ground frame in the foreground, with the Up starter pulled off in the distance. The Down side siding stands empty. Three bicycles are propped against the station building, although it is possible they were receiving attention at the hands of Andrew Jones, who was a first class mechanic, and put the long periods of inactivity to good use for the community. *Norman Jones*

(centre). **Gwyddelwern. 19th May 1961.** The single line token equipment was housed in the station office, in common with most branch line staff token stations. Here two large Webb & Thompson stand in somewhat spartan surroundings. Notice the lever collars on the shelf, and covers to protect the instruments if 'blockng back'. The 'sending key' is on the right below the commutator knobs. Train staffs were stored in the slots in the base of the instruments, just visible on the right hand column, whilst a staff has been released from the frame for the section to Ruthin. On the wall behind the further instrument can be seen the circuit telephone with the call-up code details resting on the case in its own small frame. On the office desk, the Train Register, below the 'tell-tale' signal light indicators behind. Weekly and other notices were on display, held by the inevitable bulldog clip. Despite the austere appearance, these offices were frequently very cosy retreats, heated by stoves fuelled by illicit steam coal from the engines that passed. *Norman Jones*

(lower). **Gwyddelwern. 14th May 1958.** Activity at Gwyddelwern. LMS Standard Class 2 2-6-0 No.**46433** waits at the platform with the return daily freight from Corwen to Denbigh. In the Up Goods loop, ex.Midland Railway Class 4F 0-6-0 No.**43981** waits at the head of an Engineer's Special for the section to clear before the work can be resumed. *J. Spencer Gilkes.*

Derwen. 5th May 1961, The station had changed little in the eight years since the line lost its regular passenger services, although the Down side goods loop had been severed and cut back to form a short siding, used mainly by the local coal merchant. The station building was of different design to others on the line, and retained its canopy over the station offices until the line closed permanently. Beyond the station at the Ruthin end was a small cattle dock where another siding trailed off the Up direction. The building survives to this day as a private residence and is little changed structurally, although the area under the canopy was converted to a conservatory.   *D. Thompson.*

Derwen

Derwen station was 2 miles 1297 yards from Gwyddelwern and 2 miles 121 yards from Nantclwyd. The station buildings, located on the Up side, were of different design to others on the DR&C but to date, no reason has been forthcoming for this variation. The building was more square and had a canopy built into the structure at the Corwen end. There was some local freight traffic, mainly agricultural, as well as the local coal merchant receiving a wagon load of coal twice a week. Although not a token exchange point, a goods loop was provided on the Down side, which was cut back to form a trailing siding on the Down side after regular passenger services ceased. A trailing siding in the Up direction was located north of the station, leading to a landing dock. This was removed some time before all traffic ceased. Access to the loop and siding was controlled by the train staff.

Derwen. c.1962. Taken from the platform looking towards Corwen showing the overbridge, with the coal merchant bagging up his stock for local delivery. The station offices have an air of dereliction about them although the house was still occupied.
Lens of Sutton

(left). **Derwen. 24th February 1961.** Photographs of the Ruthin end of Derwen station are comparatively rare, hence this slightly blurred photograph of the station, taken from the footplate of the returning daily freight train from Corwen. The short siding to the cattle dock has been lifted, but the small goods office was intact.

Norman Jones

(centre). **Derwen. Thursday 13th August 1953.** Despite the fact that regular passenger services had finished six months earlier, Henry Casserley was able to take this photograph of the station from the last coach of the North Wales Radio Land Cruise train as it climbed towards Gwyddelwern. The Down goods loop is still intact, and the short siding on the Up side is clearly visible.

The late H.C. Casserley.

(right). **Derwen. 24th February 1961.** The approach to Derwen station was on a gradual curve on the falling gradient, and speed was checked all the way. Just visible in the distance is the road overbridge which stood at the Corwen end of the station.

Norman Jones

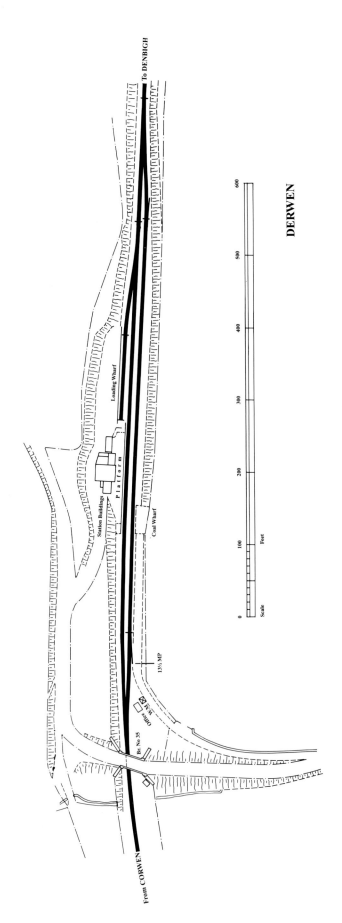

DERWEN

Scale Feet

0 100 200 300 400 500 600

To DENBIGH

From CORWEN

Loading Wharf

Station Buildings

Platform

Coal Wharf

13¾ MP

W M Office

Br. No 35

Nantclwyd. 31st January 1953. Stanier 2-6-4T No.**42568** of Chester shed at the head of the 10.25am from Chester to Corwen pauses at Nant Clwyd on the last Saturday of regular passenger traffic between Ruthin and Corwen. These large tank engines were infrequent performers on the line, and the more powerful engine was substituted for the occasion in the belief that there may be an influx of enthusiasts wishing to travel. However, apart from one person on the platform, there is little other sign of activity here and few, if any other enthusiasts travelled on this working. The station building is similar in design to that at Gwyddelwern. The gated siding was used by a local coal merchant as well as being used as a loading bank.   *W.A. Camwell*

Nantclwyd

The station was 2 miles 121 yards from Derwen and 3 miles 52 yards from Eyarth. The station buildings were on the Down side, and were of similar design to Eyarth and Gwyddelwern. It was a token exchange point until passenger services were withdrawn in 1953. The tokens were described in the Sectional Appendix as '*of special make*': those for the section to Gwyddelwern coloured red, whilst the ones for the section to Ruthin were coloured blue. In common with other stations on the line, a passing loop was provided on the Up side, but a note attached to the Working Time Tables stated that passenger trains could not cross here, or at Gwyddelwern. (A passenger train could cross a goods train, provided the goods train was in the loop line).

Facilities at the station consisted of the usual offices, booking facilities and Station Masters accommodation, etc. The train staff equipment was located in the station office. There was a reasonable amount of freight traffic, consisting mainly of agricultural produce and domestic coal. The coal yard siding was located at the Corwen end of the station, making a trailing connection and was normally gated across the line before and after use. It was the guard's duty to ensure that the gate was returned to this position after shunting. Another siding was shown on the side strip, (dated 1926), off the main line, but this had been removed before 1953. The loop at the Ruthin end of the line was extended back into a short siding and ended at a set of bufferstops. When Nantclwyd ceased to be a staff token point, the goods loop was taken out, although the coal siding remained in use until the end.

(left). Nantclwyd. 19th May 1961. The days of the daily Class **K** freight were numbered, and the slow lumbering goods train, dropping off the solitary wagon were fast disappearing. Here Fireman Emrys Ingleby works the ground frame to permit a solitary wagon of coal to be propelled into the siding behind the station building. Nant Clwyd was an idyllic spot, no road traffic nearby, with only the simmering of the Class 3F 0-6-0 boiler to disturb the peace and tranquillity.
Norman Jones.

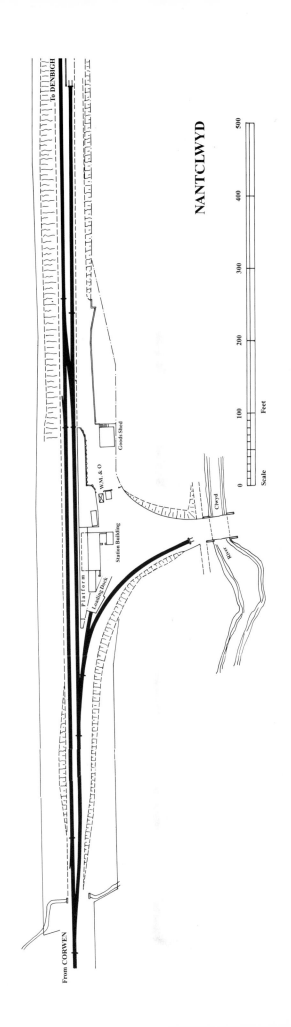

(right). Nantclwyd. 19th May 1961. The wagon of coal is safely installed in the yard behind the station, and the locomotive has drawn forward back onto the main line, allowing the siding gates to be closed. Meanwhile the guard's brake van stands alongside the platform, awaiting the return of the rest of the train. After coupling up, and ensuring that everything is in a fit state, the train will proceed towards Corwen at a leisurely pace. The passing loop has long since been lifted, although the loading gauge stands in isolation beyond the platform at the Ruthin end. Notice too, the abrupt change of gradient. *Norman Jones*

NANTCLWYD

To DENBIGH

Goods Shed

W.M. & O

Station Building

Platform

Loading Dock

Clwyd

River

From CORWEN

0   100   200   300   400   500

Feet

Scale

(upper left). **Near Eyarth**. 23rd August 1961. Taken from the Cambrian Radio Land Cruise, approaching Eyarth gorge, where the road, rail and river compete for space within the barrow confines. *Author's collection*

(upper right). **Near Eyarth. 23rd August 1961.** A hundred yards on, the track swings through a tight set of curves as it skirts the river.

Author's collection

(lower left). **Near Eyarth. 23rd August 1961.** The undulating ground level meant that one minute the track was raised on an embankment, and next it was dominated by rock face, running in a cutting. As the train approaches the gorge, this change in levels is apparent. Notice too the old "SLOW at major Road Ahead" sign, with its distinctive inverted triangle inside a circle. At the road junction, a Ford 'Popular' keeps company with a Morris 'Minor' van. Notice too the 40mph speed restriction for Corwen bound trains beyond the bridge over the stream. *Author's collection.*

(lower right). **Eyarth Gorge. n.d.** When constructing the line, it was necessary to hack a way through solid rock to negotiate the gorge. Over the years, weathering of the jagged rocks smoothed the side, whilst vegetation and growth concealed the scars somewhat. Nevertheless the track had to negotiate a path through, which caused speed restrictions to be imposed on trains in either direction. This view was taken some twenty years earlier.

J.M. Dunn.

(left). **Eyarth. 19th May 1961.** The branch scene encapsulated. The pick-up goods standing on the main line, a solitary wagon of coal for a local merchant being unloaded onto the lineside. The guard, Arthur Davies stands on the platform, whilst Driver Bill Jones surveys the scene from his lofty vantage point on the footplate. Locomotive No.**43916** of Rhyl shed wears a grimy coat, and the first British Railways emblem, sometimes referred to as the 'Ferret and Dartboard' is just visible through the grime. *Norman Jones*

(right). **Between Eyarth and Nantclwyd. 19th May 1961.** One of the charming features of the pick up goods was the ability to stop in section for a variety of purposes, mostly official, but on the odd occasion, for purely private reasons. In this instance, however, everything was legal and above board, the stop made to pick up one of the permanent way staff who had been coppice-ing on the lineside, and seen here having his bundle of stakes loaded onto the brake van verandah by Arthur Davies, the guard. Notice the cast concrete bunker with small chippings used for packing the permanent way, and the way the lineside vegetation has been cut back to the boundary fences or walls. *Norman Jones*

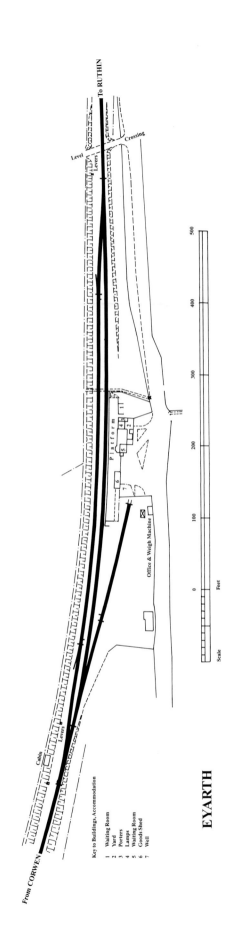

EYARTH

Key to Buildings, Accommodation

1 Waiting Room
2 Yard
3 Porters
4 Lamps
5 Waiting Room
6 Goods Shed
7 Well

From CORWEN

To RUTHIN

Cabin

Levers

Level Crossing

Levers

Platform

Office & Weigh Machine

Scale   Feet
0   100   200   300   400   500

Eyarth. 31st January 1953. On this last Saturday of regular passenger trains between Corwen and Ruthin, a 2-6-4T pulls away from Eyarth station with the 11.10am from Corwen. The poster boards, still sporting their LMS origins five years after Nationalisation have been stripped of information. Wall mounted oil lamps provide the only illumination for the low height platform and there appears to be no trace of a station nameboard. The stationmaster stands in the door of the office, presumably he had not been inundated with passengers. The station was not a block post, but the station limits were protected by signals. The Up Goods loop was latterly little used and was lifted some time before complete closure. *W.A. Camwell.*

Eyarth

Although provided with a goods loop the station was not a token exchange post, merely an intermediate halt between Ruthin and Nantclwyd. There was a certain amount of commuter traffic from here to Ruthin during the last war, but this diminished as bus services increased. Located 3 miles 52 yards from Nantclwyd and 1 mile 1394 yards from Ruthin, the station had a short siding at the Corwen end where the local coal merchant unloaded his wagons or the occasional van was placed. Freight traffic otherwise consisted mainly of agricultural produce, and some livestock.

K 158

LONDON MIDLAND AND SCOTTISH RAILWAY

SUMMER PROGRAMME

OF

EXCURSIONS

FROM

RHUDDLAN	RUTHIN
ST. ASAPH	EYARTH
TREFNANT	NANTCLWYD
DENBIGH	DERWEN
LLANRHAIADR	GWYDDELWERN
RHEWL	CORWEN

July 4th to September 25th, 1938

L M S

K 158 (3500)   21330—Swale, Widnes

Eyarth. 1930's. The station, looking towards Corwen, showing little alteration from the LNWR days, and apart from the removal of the station nameboards, which were probably removed during the second World War, and remained in this condition until passenger services were withdrawn in 1953. Notice also the low height platforms. The building design was similar to that at Nant Clwyd and Gwyddelwern, except for the absence of a canopy. *D. Thompson.*

(lower left). **Eyarth. 19th May 1961.** In order to work the point to gain access to the siding, it was first necessary to insert the train staff for the section into the two lever ground fame, which then enabled the point lock and point levers to be thrown. Here, Emrys Ingleby inserts the staff for the section from Ruthin to Nant Clwyd into the LNWR Webb design lever frame prior to working the points. *Norman Jones.*

(lower right). **Eyarth. 19th May 1961.** What traffic was handled at Eyarth and other stations in the final year of operation amounted to no more than the twice weekly wagon of coal for the local merchant, and did not require the services of a resident porter signalman. Access to the sidings was controlled by the train staff for the section, carried on the locomotive, and it fell to the fireman to unlock the frame and operate the points, whilst the guard attended to the coupling or uncoupling of the wagons and securing in their correct location on the siding. Here, Fireman Emrys Ingleby is ready to move the points over to enable the train to set back into the siding. Notice too the permanent way hut, the whitewash wearing thin and exposing the brickwork underneath.. *Norman Jones*

Ruthin. c.1949. Ruthin station was intended to be the Headquarters of the Denbigh, Ruthin & Corwen Railway, and built itself a large and imposing station, as befitted the status of the Headquarters in the former Denbighshire county town. The main platform was on the Up side, and is seen here in the second year of Nationalisation, having recently been repainted after six years of neglect during World War Two. Most trains used the Up platform which ever direction they were travelling, except where passenger trains were required to cross, which was infrequent. Nevertheless the Down platform was provided with some protection from the elements, although there was no covered accommodation for the passenger, who had had to brave the elements on the open footbridge to gain the platform in the first instance, and was probably soaked by the time the shelter was reached anyway. Notice the ornate and matching bargeboards, the design of which was alleged to be exclusive to Ruthin. Behind the Down platform was a Goods Loop line which was rarely used, and off which was an unloading dock. *L.G.R.P.No.19237*

Ruthin

As the county town for Denbighshire, the station attracted reasonable levels of passenger traffic, which justified its retention as the passenger traffic terminus, after regular services to Corwen were discontinued in 1953. The town is located in the centre of a very fertile agricultural community and its livestock markets together with other freight trade, ensured that there was sufficient traffic to warrant at least two freight train workings every day except Sundays, which persisted almost until the line closed completely to all traffic.

The station building as built had been the intended Headquarters of the Denbigh, Ruthin & Corwen Railway, reflected in its design. However the line was absorbed by the LNWR after a comparatively brief independent life and the offices were surplus to requirements. It was reputed to be a cold building and the appointment to the station (and living quarters) was possibly not quite as welcome as one might imagine.

The station consisted of a main platform, on the Up side, with a second platform on the Down, which was only used when the Up platform was occupied, both lines signalled for two way running. Passenger access was via an open footbridge across the tracks at the Corwen end of the station. The footbridge also formed part of a public right of way. A barrow crossing was located at the Denbigh end. The Down platform was rather narrow, and limited protection was provided with an open fronted shelter and overhanging canopy. A goods loop ran behind the Down platform, and a short trailing

siding off this led to a landing platform.

A locomotive depot was established here from the commencement of services, but this had closed by the turn of the century. On the 25 inch to 1 mile relevant 1883 Ordnance Survey map, the goods shed was shown as the locomotive depot, but no documentary evidence has survived to support or disprove this.

The goods yard was on the Up side at the Denbigh end, and handled a considerable volume of traffic including timber and agricultural produce, as well as handling substantial quantities of domestic coal. Movement within station limits was controlled from a small signal cabin on the Down platform, where the single line token equipment for Nantclwyd and Denbigh was located.

After regular passenger traffic to Corwen ceased in 1953, trains terminated at Ruthin and the Down platform was rarely used. Consequently the open shelter was removed. The Down loop was used for running round purposes, although the daily Corwen freight, which shunted in the goods yard for a while then drew up and stood in the Down platform road for a short while before proceeding, and again on returning.

The LMS Country Lorry service was based here, covering all the intermediate stations and the district to Corwen and surrounding villages. Before, and immediately after the Second World War, four three-ton open platform lorries worked from here and were an integral part of the service. This was hived off to the British Road Services upon Nationalisation.

(upper). **Ruthin. c.1933.** Five coach trains of bogie stock in a working takes some investigating. The train was the 4.30pm to Denbigh and Rhyl, and normally comprised of two-coach set 821. However, on Thursdays and Saturdays, the working was strengthened by including two-coach set 829, which was detached at Denbigh. On Saturdays Only, strengthening set 844 - a Third, which was a spare vehicle at Denbigh, was added to the formation and worked through to Rhyl with set 821. The train loco was replaced at Denbigh. The last vehicle is not carrying a tail lamp, so presumably traffic operations are not yet completed. Note, also, the board above the buffers reading *'Llandudno District No.2'*, a practice dating back to LNWR times, but which fell out of favour in the 1930's. The reason for the vehicle in the Down goods loop line is uncertain, but not uncommon for short term parking. Notice the edge of the loading dock.

J.P. Richards.

Ruthin. May 1947. Taken from the footbridge at the Corwen end of the station, looking towards Denbigh. The buildings and signal posts are in need of a lick of paint. The platform is devoid of passengers - as usual, although the goods yard has several vehicles awaiting action. The Down 'island' platform is seen to good advantage here, and its narrow width is apparent. Off the Down Goods loop, running behind the platform is the short siding leading to the landing dock. Access for road vehicles was over the barrow ramp under the footbridge. The signal box on the Down platform is totally obscured by the platform canopy, but its position can be determined by the ramp in the six foot.

G.H. Platt

(upper). **Ruthin. 10th September 1959.** The exterior of Ruthin station must have been imposing when it was first constructed, but it's demotion from Company headquarters to a secondary branch line station before the line opened was rapid. The former offices became the living accommodation for the Station master, but by all accounts, it was a cold residence, and only the close proximity of regular supplies of loco coal made some concession to comfort. It is significant that although the yard is full of cars, most were merely parking for convenience, and in all probability the income from this provided a significant proportion of the station's receipts in its final years. Crosville buses from Mold used to terminate here, and the author spent many short breaks between trips talking to staff on the platform. Alas, all has now disappeared and a road traffic roundabout now graces the spot.   *Norman Jones.*

(lower). **Ruthin. 10th September 1959.** Following the withdrawal of regular passenger services beyond Ruthin to Corwen in 1953, most trains from Chester and, until the Vale of Clwyd line also lost it's regular passenger service, from Rhyl, terminated at Ruthin. There was sufficient commuter traffic to justify the retention of passenger services between here and Denbigh. Two or three coaches sufficed, almost exclusively non corridor stock, as it had never been the practice to run through coaches beyond Chester or Rhyl. The easy gradients meant that Class 2 locomotives were adequate for most passenger services, and here BR Standard Class 2 2-6-0 No.**78038** with Driver E. Evans at the regulator together with his fireman pose for the photographer, who had shared the cab from Denbigh.   *Norman Jones.*

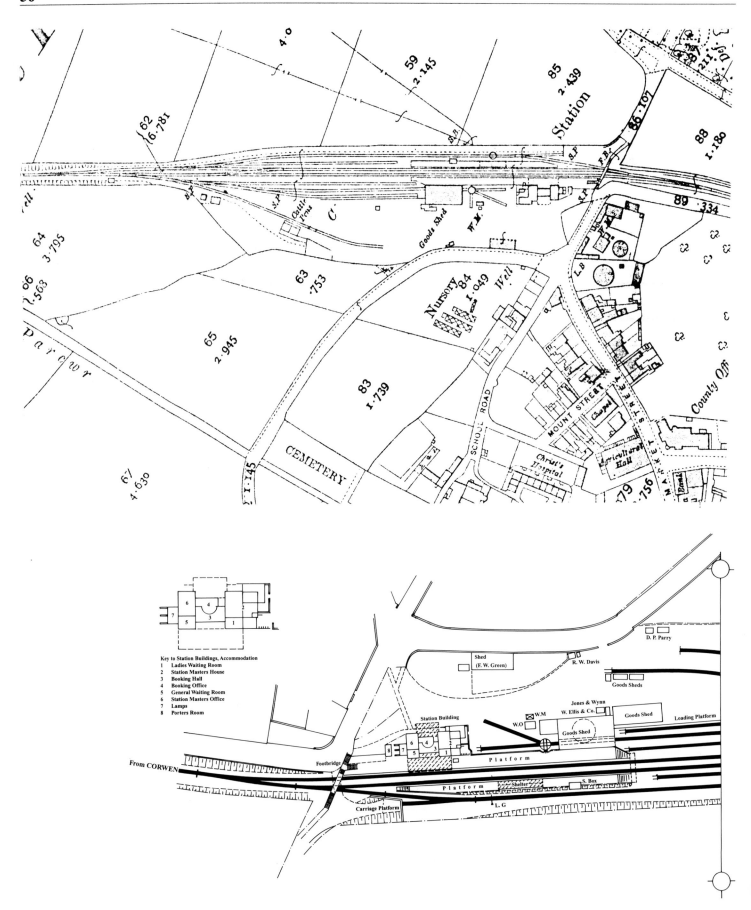

Key to Station Buildings, Accommodation
1 Ladies Waiting Room
2 Station Masters House
3 Booking Hall
4 Booking Office
5 General Waiting Room
6 Station Masters Office
7 Lamps
8 Porters Room

Ruthin. 10th September 1959. In common with many stations on the former Denbigh, Ruthin and Corwen line, the platform faces were faced in local stone, and were rather low, necessitating portable steps for the less agile passengers. Here, Class 3F 0-6-0 No.**43618**,returning from Corwen, pauses in the Down loop line at the station, whilst BR Standard Class 2 2-6-0 No.**78038** stands at the Up side platform with the stock forming the 3.00pm to Chester. Once the passenger has cleared Denbigh, the freight will continue its leisurely pace to Denbigh. Notice the small signal cabin. The former Down platform looks singularly bare after the canopy and shelter were removed.   *Norman Jones*

RUTHIN

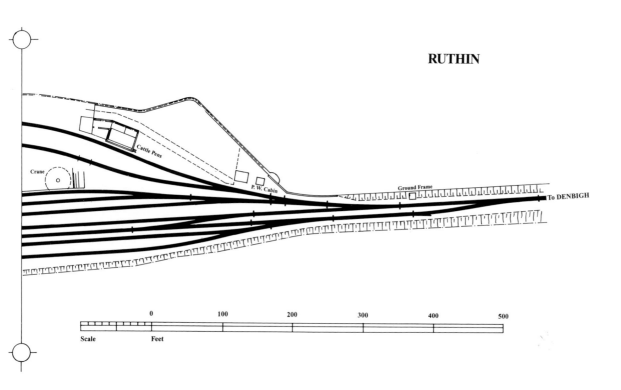

(upper). **Ruthin. 10th September 1959.** Another view of Ruthin signal cabin. The box housed a 22 lever frame of which 15 were working levers, and were listed as LNW Tumbler type. In true railwayman tradition, the staff created and tended flower beds in their slack times, and in this case, extended to a small bird bath, although it looks suspiciously like an adaption from something more utilitarian. Porter Signalman R. Williams observes the proceedings.   *Norman Jones*

(lower left). **Ruthin. 19th May 1961.** Guard Arthur Davies gives the 'right away' signal to Driver Bill Jones and Fireman Emrys Ingleby, on the footplate of Class 3F 0-6-0 No.**43618,** working the 8.10am Class **K** freight to Corwen, seen departing from the Down platform line, observed by members of the station staff. Progress was very leisurely. Arrival at Ruthin was 8.30am, and the next 90 minutes were spent shunting in the yard prior to a 10.00am departure for the hills.   *Norman Jones*

(lower right). **Ruthin. Friday 24th February 1961.** Staff pose for the photographer in front of Ruthin signal box. The gentleman on the left hand side is unknown, believed to be the Station Foreman. Between him and Porter Signalman R. Williams standing in the box doorway is the Guard of the Corwen freight, the late Arthur Davies.   *Norman Jones.*

(upper). **Ruthin. 10th September 1959.** Signalman R. Williams with an unnamed colleague stand on either side of the miniature train staff instrument inside Ruthin signal box. The instrument was for the section to Denbigh, and replaced a large Webb & Thompson token instrument. Notice the standard fittings that typified the country signal box, the large clock, the ceiling suspended gas lamp, the vintage circuit telephone with the working timetable open at the relevant page, the desk, with the Train Register open at the current page and calender above. The standard LNW levers in the foreground are highly polished, and probably a duster was held to prevent sweat staining the hand grip. The country signalbox on the branch line was a way of life that has disappeared from the community, and we are the losers by their passing.
Norman Jones

(lower). **Ruthin. Thursday 10th September 1959.** BR Standard Class 2 2-6-0 No.**78038** having detached from the stock, runs round the coaches, through the Down loop line, passing the signalbox. Driver E. Evans at the regulator.   *Norman Jones.*

(upper). **Ruthin. 10th September 1959.** Another view of Class 3F 0-6-0 No.**43618** standing alongside BR Standard Class 2 No.**78038**.

Norman Jones.

(centre). **Ruthin. 10th September 1959.** The stock off the 10.25am from Chester stand in the main platform at Ruthin. On weekdays there was a long layover time here, and the locomotive was utilised for shunting in the goods yard as required. After regular passenger services to Corwen were withdrawn in February 1953, the former goods loop line that ran behind the Down platform was severed and made into a trailing siding, terminating in these stops against which a brake van stands. Although the loco has not yet returned from shunting, the signalman on the morning turn walks down the ramp with the hoop carrying the single line token pouch for the section Ruthin to Denbigh over his shoulder. Departure time must be imminent.

Norman Jones.

(lower). **Ruthin. 10th September 1959.** Ruthin goods yard was always busy, as befitted a Market town, and limited siding space meant that it was necessary to shunt the yard for most of the day to position wagons and avoid blockage and delay. Here BR standard Class 2 No.**78038** on layover time from passenger duties draws empty mineral wagons out of the coal siding and positions them ready for the returning Corwen to Denbigh freight to work forward.   *Norman Jones*

(upper). **Ruthin. 9th May 1949.** Another view of the Down platform shelter, taken from a Corwen train. Beyond the shelter is Ruthin signal box. Behind the platform is the Down Goods Loop line, with a loading gauge bereft of the suspended clearance bar looking like a gibbet. Notice the ornate gas lamp and station name board. *E.S. Russell.*

(lower right). **Ruthin Goods Yard. 24th February 1961.** A once familiar scene that has all but disappeared forever. Shunting taking place in Ruthin yard on a dismal wet morning. Guard Arthur Davies rests his shunter pole on the ground whilst another unknown guard controls a setting back movement with hand signals. In the background, coalmen load sacks off the ground. *Norman Jones*

(lower left). **Ruthin. 10th September 1959.** Taken from the footplate of No.**78038** waiting to depart with the 3.00pm Class B passenger train from Ruthin to Chester, looking towards Denbigh. Alongside is No.**43618**, pausing on the Down loop line after working the daily freight from Corwen, and when the passenger train has cleared the section, will follow it to Denbigh. *Norman Jones*

Rhewl. n.d. This early view from the minor road overbridge shows the station in the early years of the century, if the dress of the three ladies is anything to go by. There are the usual display of advertising signs, but the view has been included because it shows the canopy over the platform.   *Lens of Sutton*

Rhewl

1 mile 794 yards and four minutes running time from Ruthin, Rhewl station was on the Up side of the line, which ran in more or less a straight line along the valley floor. At one time the station boasted a canopy to protect the passengers, but this was removed about 1950. The station enjoyed sufficient patronage to justify its remaining open to traffic when the passenger traffic beyond Ruthin ceased. The line passed under a minor road bridge and a goods loop was provided on the Down side, although the station was not a token exchange point, and the loop was little used and eventually the southern connection was removed, forming a long siding. There was also a small goods yard on the Up side served by a trailing connection. The station buildings survive to this day, and despite having been extensively renovated are easily identifiable.

Rhewl. 5th May 1961. The line from Ruthin to Denbigh cut across the valley floor more or less in a straight line. First stop out of Ruthin was Rhewl, where the line passed under a minor road bridge before running into the station, the platform and buildings being on the Up side. At one time there was a canopy over the platform, but this was removed when the services from Ruthin to Corwen were withdrawn. The sidings on either side of the running line appear to be little used.   *D. Thompson.*

Rhewl. 1961. This view of Rhewl was taken by former member of Denbighshire County Council staff, and sadly the negative has been lost, the only surviving print being rather small. Nevertheless it shows the station from the Denbigh end, and shows two fuel tankers on the Down side siding, together with the landing dock siding on the Up side. The yard was out of use and overgrown. The station buildings and bridge survive and the course of the railway is still easy to follow.

Clwyd County Council.

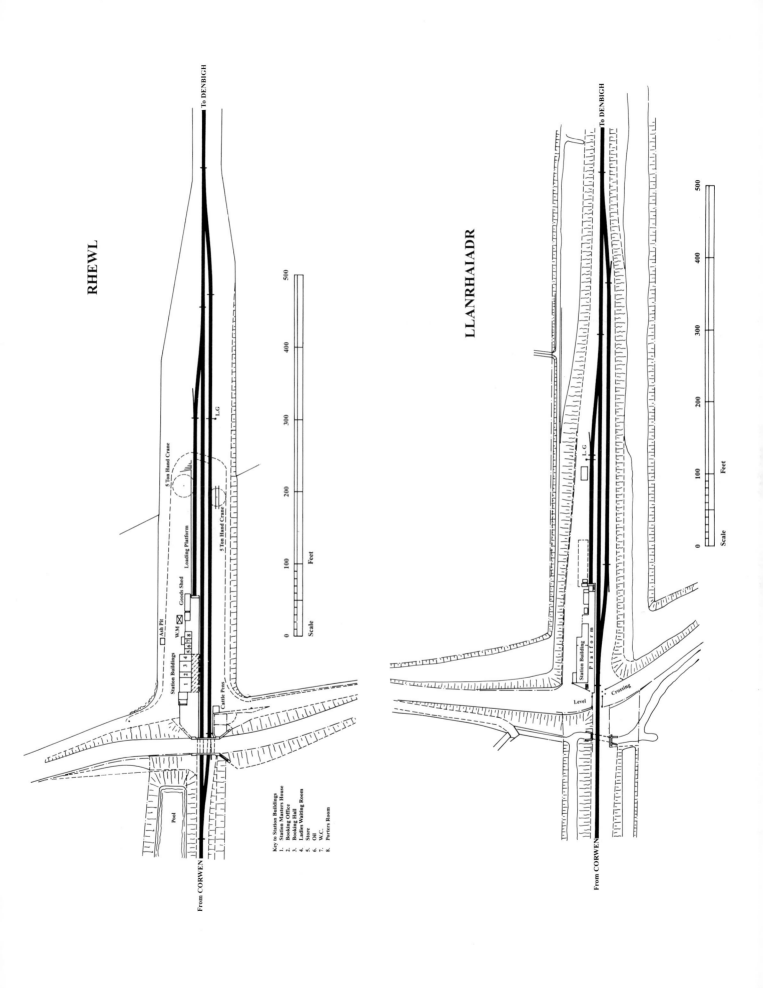

RHEWL

To DENBIGH

5 Ton Hand Crane

L.G

5 Ton Hand Crane

Loading Platform

Ash Pit

Station Buildings

W.M

Goods Shed

1 2 3 4 5 6 7 8

Cattle Pens

Pool

From CORWEN

Key to Station Buildings
1. Station Masters House
2. Booking Office
3. Booking Hall
4. Ladies Waiting Room
5. Store
6. Oil
7. W.C.
8. Porters Room

Scale

0   100   200   300   400   500

Feet

LLANRHAIADR

To DENBIGH

L-G

Station Building

Platform

Level   Crossing

From CORWEN

Scale

0   100   200   300   400   500

Feet

Llanrhaiadr. n.d. LMS Class 2P 4-4-0 No.**40671** pauses briefly at Llanrhaiadr with the 10.25am from Chester to Corwen, comprised of two non corridor coaches. The station was some way from the village, consequently trains were poorly patronised and the station closed to passenger traffic in February 1953, although it remained open for parcels and freight traffic, mainly because of the need to man the level crossing. Latterly the station, in a run-down condition and in need of a coat of paint, was a gloomy looking structure and the canopy, which was removed after closure, although providing some protection in wet weather, overshadowed the station building and did nothing to improve the atmosphere.
W.A. Camwell.

Railway Station, Llanrhaiadr, near Denbigh

(lower). **Llanrhaiadr.** A commercial postcard produced in the early part of this century shows the station in a better light, mainly because it was in a well maintained state. It is presumed that the group on the platform are the families of the station staff, and it would seem that these comprised the Station Master, nearest the camera, a porter, a ganger and a booking clerk. There was some freight traffic, but not enough to justify a goods shed. One of the station buildings sufficed. *Jim Peden collection.*

Llanrhaiadr. 31st January 1953. Formalities over, 4-4-0 No.**40671** of Rhyl (6K) shed pulls away from rest, the fireman looking back to check that the train is following and all is in order. The poster board on the side of the station building still sports 'LMS' five years after it ceased to exist, but was removed shortly after.
W.A. Camwell

Llanrhaiadr

About half way between Ruthin and Denbigh is Llanrhaiadr, a sizeable community. Nevertheless the station was some way from the village, and local patronage was poor, so much so that the station was closed to passenger traffic in February 1953. A minor road crossed the line on the level, and it was necessary to retain a staff presence to work the hand operated level crossing gates. The same individual dealt with what parcels and freight traffic came their way. The station building was located on the Up side, and was similar to Rhewl; at one time it boasted a canopy but this was removed in 1953. There was a small lever frame at the southern end of the platform that controlled the signals protecting the crossing, and operated the foot passenger gate lock. At one time the complex had a goods loop on the Down side, and also a trailing siding on the Up, which terminated behind the short platform. The loop was lifted in 1953 but had been out of use for some time. Like Rhewl, the station was not a staff token station, merely an intermediate halt.

Today the station buildings have gone, the site has been used to store County Council road mending materials, but the course of the line is still clearly visible

Llanrhaiadr. c.1959. Although the passenger service from the station had been withdrawn some years previously, it was necessary to have staff in attendance throughout the day to operate the hand operated level crossing gates, and in between times, deal with parcels and freight traffic. The gates were protected by signals, and a small lever frame was located between the station building and the road. The frame platform and protecting posts are just visible to the right of the picture. Night time illumination was provided by the wall mounted oil lamp.
Norman Jones.

(upper). **Denbigh. c.1921.** Passenger services in LNWR days between Denbigh, Ruthin and Corwen were mainly in the hands of 2-4-2T locomotives, which obviated the need to turn the locomotives, and avoid paying the Great Western Railway for the use of their turntable at Corwen. Here, an unidentified loco approaches Denbigh with a train of six 6-wheel coaches from Ruthin.

Author's collection.

(lower). **Denbigh. c.1921.** Another unidentified 2-4-2T draws away from Denbigh past Fron fields with a train of seven 6-wheel coaches bound for Corwen. The town of Denbigh stands out starkly against the backdrop of the fields and hillside. The smokebox of the loco shows signs of scorching, possibly the door was warped, admitting air. These little locomotives were thrashed by their drivers who took pride in running to time, or making up any lost, if at all possible. Even on branch lines, the timings were surprisingly tight.

Author's collection

(upper). **Denbigh. c.1919.** Denbigh station was built into a gradual slope, and the platforms were some twenty feet above the natural ground level, mainly because the railway had to cross Vale Street, and give adequate clearance for road traffic. Consequently the southern approach to Denbigh necessitated climbing from the valley floor about a mile after leaving Llanrhaiadr. The final approach to Denbigh was on a gradient of 1 in 63. South-bound trains, once on the move, rolled down the slope, for most of the way. Here a Denbigh based 2-4-2T with six 6-wheel coaches coasts past Fron fields en route for Ruthin. In the background, the stark gash of the Craig limestone quarry dominates the landscape. *Author's collection*

(lower). **Denbigh. 15th July 1920.** A Royal visit was an event to be celebrated at any time, and visits by the reigning monarch to the principality were and still are, comparatively rare occurrences. Consequently on the occasion that King George V visited Denbigh, the town put on its best appearance and ensured that everything went off without a hitch. The Royal Train was drawn by two 4-4-0 locomotives, numbers alas not recorded, and the train is seen here drawn up at Denbigh station. Notice the police presence on the skyline by the bridge, and the ganger on the down side. The fireman in the leading engine leans out of the cab to get a better view. *Author's collection*

(upper). **Denbigh. Thursday 8th September 1960.** BR Standard Class 4 4-6-0 No. **75054** of Rhyl (6K) shed coasts up the gradient past Fron fields into Denbigh station with the last 'Welsh Chieftain' working of the season comprising the usual six coaches, some carrying the coach boards above the windows, and the Observation Car bringing up the rear. These locomotives made short work of the job, and replaced the LMS Class 2 Ivatt design that commenced these workings at the commencement of the decade.

Author's collection

(centre). **Denbigh. 25th September 1960.** The Up direction home signal protecting Denbigh station looking towards Ruthin. The smaller arms below the home signal were lowered to permit trains that required to set back into the platform or the loop line. Notice the abrupt change of gradient beyond bridge no. 2. over Park Street.

Author's collection

(lower). **Denbigh. 20th August 1966.** The line passed over Park Street at this point, on the south side of Denbigh. The bridge was constructed of local limestone from the nearby Graig Quarries. Notice the old style 'Low Bridge' sign, declaring its limited headroom clearance. *Author's collection*

(upper). **Denbigh. 26th May 1947.** LMS 2-4-2T No.**6650** of Rhyl (7D) shed stands at the head of the 10.40am Chester to Corwen at the south end of Denbigh station. Further up the platform is the stock for the 11.10am Corwen (12.05pm from Denbigh) to Chester, and across the platform in the bay is the stock for the 12.10pm to Rhyl. Between No.2 signal box and the station building can be seen a 'fire devil', used to keep the water column from freezing up. Notice, too, the ornate station lamp and LMS station nameboard. *W.A. Camwell*

Denbigh. 25th September 1960. The single through platform at Denbigh caused minor complications when it became necessary for two trains travelling in opposite directions to use the same line. The procedure was for trains travelling to Mold and Chester from Ruthin to pull into the platform, where cross platform transfers to the Vale of Clwyd line and Rhyl took place. Meanwhile, trains heading to Ruthin and Corwen from Mold would run thorough the loop line and set back into the platform face. Two minutes were allowed for this purpose, and a note was made to this effect on the Working Time Tables.

Author's collection

(upper). **Denbigh. 10th September 1959.** One of the perennial tasks for the enginemen was to top up the tanks with water, sometimes a pleasant enough task, especially on warm sunny days, but less attractive on cold winter nights, by the light of dim yard lamps. However, on this occasion, Driver E.Evans stands by the water valve wheel whilst his mate keeps a watchful eye on the level in the tank. The tower of Denbigh Gas Works castellated tower, now demolished, can be seen over the cab roof. *Norman Jones*

(lower). **Denbigh. 10th September 1959.** Driver E. Evans surveys the scene from the cab of BR Standard Class 2 No.**78038** prior to working tender first to Corwen with the daily freight turn. *Norman Jones*

Denbigh. 23rd April 1959. Rhyl based engine No.**46445** awaits departure time with the 3.22pm for Chester. Having left Ruthin at 3.00pm, the timetable allowed an eight minute stopover when the Mold Junction men were relieved by a Rhyl traincrew at Denbigh for this all stations train that would take just over one and a half hours for the 36 miles, with calls at all but Star Crossing on the eastbound journey. The days in North Wales of this Ivatt 2-6-0 however were numbered and she was shortly to be transferred to Rugby on 20th June 1959. Readers will note that it has been necessary to draw the engine ahead of the signal to enable replenishment with water of the tender, no doubt passengers arriving late being given ample time to make their way down the platform.

R.J. Buckley.

Denbigh

Denbigh station has been covered in detail in a previous book in this series, and the author would refer readers to that work.

The station occupied a prominent position in the town, the white stone station building dominating the approach to Vale Street, its spire being a landmark for many years. Nevertheless the site was cramped and although traffic never reached congestion or saturation levels, required smart work by the traffic staff who had to supervise the movement of Corwen bound trains from Rhyl or Chester that by-passed the station before setting back into the through platform face. There are known cases cited where passengers, thinking they were not stopping at the station, attempted to get out when the train eventually stopped beyond Vale Street bridge prior to setting back.

1938 and 1939 were the busiest in the station's history, with over one hundred train movements recorded on a normal summer Saturday, excluding any excursion and additional traffic, and former staff have recounted instances when the last train to Ruthin has been extended to Nant Clwyd and even Corwen to cater for the late night passenger. The Supplement to the Special Traffic Notice for September 2nd 1939 advised staff that the 11.00pm from Chester to Denbigh was to be extended to Corwen, due 1.10am, and departing Empty Stock at 1.25am for Denbigh due 2.04am. Similarly the 11.48am from Chester, due Denbigh at 1.06am was extended to Ruthin, due there at 1.24am and returning Empty Stock to Denbigh, depart Ruthin 1.40am due Denbigh 1.57am. How different things became following the declaration of war nine hours later. The undated emergency timetables, prepared in 1938, when it seemed possible that war would come in that year, but deferred, came into operation on Sunday 11th September 1939. To say the changes were drastic is an understatement. Trains left Denbigh for Corwen at 6.43am, 9.05am, 5.12pm and 7.50pm, and journey times were extended, returning from Corwen at 8.10am, 10.50am, 6.50pm and 9.10pm. There were two additional workings between Denbigh and Ruthin, whilst the Vale of Clwyd line was reduced to seven trains each way. The belief was that there would be an exodus of staff to the forces, and that freight traffic would suddenly intensify, but these did not happen as drastically as feared, and by November there was a relaxation of the 40mph limit on timings and a small increase in some passenger services. However the LMS had made use of the situation to prune out a lot of the lightly loaded services, and after the war, the traffic services on all routes into and out of Denbigh were but a shadow of their pre-war level.

The Motive Power department at Denbigh had suffered some reduction in staffing levels in the late twenties and thirties. They had reached their peak about 1927 when there were 44 sets of men booked to the depot. Numbers had diminished to about thirty sets by the outbreak of war. Some of the work had been transferred to Rhyl under the reorganisation of the Motive Power structure. By 1945 it was reported that there were twenty two sets of men, and increasingly more work was lost or transferred away to Rhyl, Mold Junction or Chester, so that by 1954 there were only fourteen sets of men on the depot. After closure in September 1955, there were but four drivers and no firemen retained at Denbigh, which became an outstation of Rhyl. Firemen for these duties were despatched from Rhyl, sometimes by bus, and paid travelling time each way. At the close of passenger services in 1962, only two drivers remained in the residential link, and these were subsequently amalgamated into the Rhyl list.

It is understood that there were sixteen guards based at Denbigh in 1930, of which six were goods guards. There were also a couple of porter guards, but no details have survived . So far, I have been unable to trace details of the traffic and station staff at Denbigh.

Denbigh. 24th February 1961. BR Standard Class 2MT 2-6-0 No.**78056** stands on the Up and Down Loop line at Denbigh awaiting the arrival of the 7.55am from Ruthin to Chester. There is a goodly mix of rolling stock, and until the various grades of traffic handled were reduced, this was typical of freight trains, at least as far as Ruthin. The single wagon load was discouraged later in the decade which spelt the death knell of the branch line pick up goods.
Norman Jones

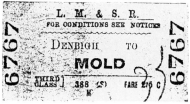

(lower).**Denbigh. n.d.** Denbigh No.2. signal cabin was located at the southern end of the station, and controlled movements at that end of the station. The box was a standard LNWR design, and housed a frame which controlled six points and seven signals. It was taken out of service when the new signal box was commissioned in 1957. It was, by all accounts, a very draughty box to work, and certainly looked on its last lags when this photograph was taken. *British Railways London Midland Region.*

To MOLD

DAY and HALF-DAY EXCURSIONS—Weekdays Also SUNDAY EXCURSIONS until September 11th

Departure Times from DENBIGH—
Day Excursions (Weekdays)—7-16, 8-14, 8-30, 9-6, 9-55, 11-45 a.m.
Half-day Excursions (Weekdays)—12-45, 1-50, 2SX25, 2SO45, 3-35 p.m.
Sunday Excursions (until Sept. 11th)—9-32 a.m.

RETURN FARES (Third Class)—
Day Excursions, 2s.8ld.   Half-day and Sundays 1s. 7d.

B—INTER-AVAILABILITY BY RAIL OR ROAD. The return halves of these tickets will be accepted for return between the same points on Crosville bus or L M S train, but in the case of the return journey being made by road, small supplementary charge will be raised. For particuars see separate announcement.

SX—Saturdays excepted.   SO—Saturdays only.
RETURN ARRANGEMENTS—Passengers return same day by any train.

To RUTHIN and CORWEN

DAY and HALF-DAY EXCURSIONS—Weekdays Also Sunday Excursions to Ruthin until Sept. 11th

FROM	DAY EXCURSIONS Weekdays					HALF-DAY Week-days	HALF-DAY Sundays until Sept. 11th		Ruthin Day	Ruthin Half-day	Corwen Day	Corwen Half-day
	A a.m.	a.m.	A a.m.	a.m.	A p.m.	p.m.	A p.m.	A p.m.	s. d.	s. d.	s. d.	s. d.
Rhuddlan	7 35	8 37	9 54	11 7	2 32	2 32	12 47	2 37	1 11	1 4	3 7	2 8
St. Asaph	7 41	8 43	10 5	11 13	2 38	2 38	12 58	2 43	1 7	1 4	3 3	2 1
Trefnant	7 48	8 50	10 12	11 20	2 47	2 47	1 10	2 50	1 4	1 1	2 11	2 1
DENBIGH	8 24	9 5	10 25	11 50	3 0	3 40	1 19	3 0	1 0	1 0	2 6	1 7

A—For Ruthin only.

RETURN ARRANGEMENTS—Passengers return same day by any train.

CORWEN to RUTHIN
HALF-DAY EXCURSIONS
Every Weekday at 1-37 p.m.
Return Fare 1/4 Third Class
Passengers return same day by any train.

(upper). **Denbigh. 1958.** The new signalbox, built to replace the old No.1 and 2 cabins on either side of the station, and Mold & Denbigh Junction, 1700 yards towards Rhyl, was commissioned week-end 4th May 1957 and was a distinct improvement, with comfortable working conditions for the men, and good visibility all round. The signalling was renewed at the same time and track circuiting was installed. The double track to Mold & Denbigh Junction was modified to two parallel single lines, the former Up line becoming the Up and Down line to Foryd Junction, whilst the Down line became the Up and Down line to Bodfari. The old Webb & Thompson Staff Token equipment between Denbigh No.2 and Ruthin was replaced by Key Token coloured green, whilst a Key Token coloured blue was used for the section Denbigh - Bodfari. and new instruments and staffs were provided. The existing miniature staff coloured red was used for the section Denbigh - Foryd Junction although the wording was modified eliminating the wording Mold & Denbigh Junction - Foryd Junction. The siting of the new box caused the loco release road on the Down side to be slewed over into the timber yard. Sadly the box had a very short life, and when passenger services between Chester, Mold and Denbigh to Ruthin were withdrawn in 1962, the box was surplus to requirements and eventually demolished.

Jim Parry, Rhyl.

(lower). **Denbigh. n.d.** Looking more dilapidated than No.2 box, seen earlier, No.1 box was located on the Up side between the running lines and the Up side sidings and goods yard. It was as uncomfortable to work in as it looked, and it came as a great relief to the signalmen when the new box came into use in 1957.

British Railways London Midland Region

(upper). **Denbigh. 1923.** An LNWR 2-4-2T pollutes the atmosphere as it pulls past the shed and away from Denbigh with a working to Rhyl comprising one bogie coach and the usual circuit stock of five 6-wheel coaches. 0-6-0 No.**3136** stands at the coaling stage/water tank, the coalmen just visible through the smoke, whilst two more 2-4-2T locomotives can be seen on the Up side in the goods yard. Denbigh was a hive of activity and the freight traffic density was very heavy. Denbigh No.1. box can just be seen in the background. The goods yard headshunt extended a short distance behind the camera, and access to Graig Quarry siding to the right was off this line, level with the first coach. *Author's collection*

(lower). **Denbigh. 1923.** LNWR 2-4-0 No.**1666** *Ariadne* pulls past Denbigh shed with a Chester working, comprising the usual five coach set of 6-wheel stock and a horse box. On the loco coal siding road stands another set of six-wheeled coaches. Notice the old shed roof, which was replaced shortly after the war. *Author's collection*

(upper). **Denbigh. 19th August 1934.** For many years, Denbigh shed was independent of attachment, although never allocated its own shedcode. When the LMS was formed, however, it came under the control of Llandudno Junction, as did Rhyl. The revision of Motive Power structure, and establishment of the Concentration and Garage schemes in the mid 1930's nevertheless changed the administrative procedure, and Denbigh became a sub-shed to Rhyl. Here, two of the three locomotives visible carry the old LNW shed allocation for Llandudno Junction - Shed 38 - adorning Fowler Class 4F 0-6-0 No.**4396** and 2-4-2T No.**6602.** No.**8337** stands facing the shed. Behind the 4F is No.**5497** *Majestic.* A note on the print records that inside the shed behind 6602 were Nos.**6625, 6669, 6725,** and behind 8337 was **6611, 6680** and **8401.** *W.A. Camwell*

(centre). **Denbigh. 6th July 1935.** Another pre war view of Denbigh shed, this time viewed from across the running lines to Mold & Denbigh Junction. On shed is the same 0-6-0 as seen in the previous photograph, accompanied by No.**6615.** The shed code plates have now been changed, and presumably the locos carry **7D** plates. The building carries the LNW vents in the roof, but, according to J.M. Dunn, who formally inspected the place as part of his duties as Leading Foreman, the roof was in a poor condition then. It was destined to remain so until after the war, when the roof was replaced. *Author's collection*

(lower). **Denbigh. 22nd April 1957.** The shed was extensively rebuilt after the Second World War, but the improvements were of little benefit to the men, for the shed closed when passenger services were withdrawn from the Vale of Clwyd line in 1955. The building was occasionally used for storing stock or locomotives out of use, and the water tank and turntable were still used, as was the shed yard. Access to the turntable was along the shed road nearest the camera, with buffer stops on the far side of the table. This view was taken shortly before the new signalbox and signalling arrangements were commissioned, hence the crosses on the arms. *W.A. Camwell*

(upper). **Denbigh. 25th September 1960.** When Mold & Denbigh Junction signalbox was abolished, the signalling arrangements were altered to reflect the fact that two single lines to Foryd Junction and Bodfari replaced the former Up and Down lines. Two straight post signals, outside the Up and Down Chester and Rhyl lines were installed, 870 yards from the box. Each carried the Down Chester and Down Rhyl Outer Home signals respectively, 25 feet above rail level, and the Up Chester and Up Rhyl Advanced Starter signals respectively, five feet lower, and on the reverse sides of the posts. Track circuiting was installed, indicated by the diamond shaped sign mounted on each post. Notice too the cast concrete fog signalman's hut, a product of Newton Heath concrete works. Beyond can be seen the loco yard siding behind the shed.   *Author's collection*

(lower). **Mold & Denbigh Junction. 25th September 1960.** The parting of the ways! This was the site of the former Mold & Denbigh Junction signalbox, and the single line from Trefnant made a connection with the double line from Bodfari, worked as Up and Down to Denbigh station. When the new Denbigh Station Signalbox was commissioned in 1957 the Junction box was taken out of use and demolished. There was some track re-alignment but little else. The independent Mold & Denbigh Junction railway proposed constructing a triangular junction here with the Vale of Clwyd, but the latter were absorbed into the LNWR before construction started, and the proposal was abandoned. The LNWR then resurrected the proposal to create an avoiding line here prior to World War I so that trains from Mold could proceed directly to Rhyl, but was postponed for the duration. It was considered finally in early LMS days, but rejected.
                                                                                          Author's collection

Trefnant. 9th May 1949. Trefnant station was a squat square brick building, presenting a depressing appearance, even on bright sunny days. It was located in the centre of the village, where the roads from Henllan and Bodfari crossed the Denbigh to St.Asaph road and, which should have provided a significant amount of traffic, but failed to do. The station was a token exchange point, although traffic on the line rarely saw trains crossing. There has been a half hearted attempt to provide flower beds on the main (Up) platform.

E.S. Russell

Trefnant

Located 1 mile 1182 yards from Mold & Denbigh Junction signal box, the station was a Electric Staff Token Block station, with a passing loop and small goods yard. The main buildings were on the Up side, and consisted of an uninspired red brick structure which contained accommodation for the Station Master. There was latterly no shelter for passengers on the Down side although one is shown in the 1906 drawing. Passengers for Denbigh crossed the line by the barrow crossing at the southern end of the station or walked over the road bridge across the tracks and down steps.

The Electric Token Block instruments were located in the ticket office. The tokens were described as 'Special make', those for the section to Mold & Denbigh Junction were coloured blue, and for the section to St.Asaph was coloured red. Signals and the loop points were controlled from an 11 lever ground frame on the Up platform at the St.Asaph end of the station.

The goods yard, also on the Up side, consisted of two sidings, one of which was used by the local coal merchant, and which extended back behind the buildings almost to the yard entrance. The Railway

Clearing House *Handbook of Stations for 1929* lists the station accommodation as a Goods and Passenger & Parcels station, catering also for Live Stock, Horse boxes and prize cattle vans, carriages by passenger train, and the yard had a crane of 5 ton capacity. Cattle pens and a landing stage were provided.

Although the station was centrally placed in the village, at an intersection where roads from Henllan and Bodfari met the Denbigh to St.Asaph road, little traffic was generated from these villages. Parcels, freight and livestock provided most of the station revenue. Few passenger trains crossed at the station, and the staff led a very peaceful if uneventful life.

With the closure to passenger traffic from 19th September 1955, the station lost a part of its revenue, but the freight and parcels traffic, which contributed the major share, continued.

An ultimate consequence of the closure was the removal of the intermediate block sections on the line between Foryd Junction and Denbigh (the new station box), replaced by a single section using miniature train staff which took place on 6th July 1957, although a note in the *Weekly Temporary Speed Restrictions, Permanent Way Operations, Signal Alterations* book for the Western Division, issue W2 - No.18 dated Saturday 4th May to Friday 10th May 1957 (page 41) states that:

'Denbigh - Mold & Denbigh Junction - The signal box ceases to be a block post and the Miniature Staff Working for the section [from Mold & Denbigh Junction s.b.} to Foryd Junction is withdrawn'
A further note states:

'The single line token between Denbigh Station and Foryd Junction is worked in accordance with the Electric Token Block Regulations with Miniature Staffs, round in shape, coloured red and lettered **Denbigh - Foryd Junction** *which releases the ground frames formerly released by the Miniature Staff for the section Mold & Denbigh Junction - Foryd Junction'*. At the same time, the Down side loop at Trefnant was taken out.

The station had its excitement late in life, when on Saturday 16th September 1961 the daily freight from Rhyl, consisting of 24 wagons and vans and the obligatory brake van, whilst approaching bridge No.4 at Trefnant, suffered a mishap, causing the last six wagons to derail. The accident was attributed to a faulty stretch of track.

The station site was cleared after closure and the road overbridge removed. Today houses occupy the station site.

Between Trefnant and St.Asaph was Llanerch Siding, 1 mile 22 yards from Trefnant, on the Up side of the line, which was a private siding facing Rhyl. Originally it served a small brickworks. A second connection was installed south of the first in 1944 leading to a network of three sidings. The work was at the instigation of the military authorities, and construction was undertaken by the Royal Engineers, supervised by the railway authorities. Initially it served as a petrol, oil and lubricants depot, but other military hardware was handled. After the conflict, they were surplus to military requirements, and latterly were used to store wagons. It has been quoted elsewhere that the Royal Train was stabled here in 1949 and 10th July 1953. However, the latter is incorrect. The author has in his possession *Notice No.42W Notice of Royal Trains - Llanelly (W.R.) to Caernarvon* and *Rhyl to Wrexham (W.R.) on Friday, 10th July 1953*. The Royal Train was worked from Shrewsbury to Glan Conway on the Blaenau Ffestiniog branch, where it remained coupled to a Class 7F 0-8-0 from 3.55am until 9.05am when the train proceeded to Caernarvon under the control of two 2-6-4T engines and Bangor traincrew.

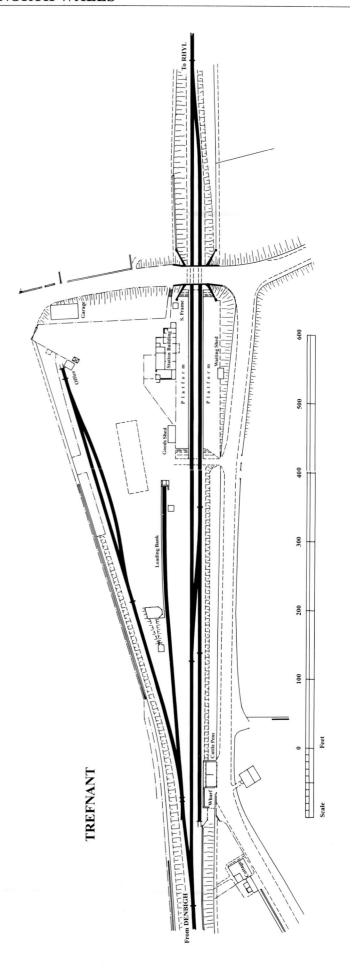

TREFNANT

(upper). **Trefnant. 27th May 1947.** LMS Compound No.**1093** sporting a 7C (Holyhead) shedplate stands at the Down platform with the 4.12pm Rhyl to Denbigh train, comprising the usual two non corridor coach formation. Compounds were not unknown over the Vale of Clwyd line, but the more normal power for this service would have been one of Rhyl shed's Class 2 engines. Quite why a Holyhead engine was working the diagram is a bit of a mystery, and it must be assumed that there had been a power failure, with this particular locomotive available. The locomotive moved to Llandudno Junction shed on 21st June 1947. *W.A. Camwell*

(centre). **Trefnant. 1956.** The station, seen from the Denbigh end and looking towards St.Asaph. The small building on the Up platform served as the goods shed, and the goods yard extended behind the station. *G.H. Platt*

(lower). **Trefnant. 1956.** Taken from the road overbridge at the north end of the station, looking towards Denbigh. The small goods yard on the Up side catered for the usual agricultural traffic and the local coal merchant also had a siding which extended behind the station. The Down platform was devoid of shelter, and there was not much provided for the Up side passengers either. *G.H. Platt.*

(upper). **St.Asaph. 6th July 1961.** BR Standard Class 4MT 4-6-0 No.**75034** pulls away from St.Asaph with the Cambrian Radio Cruise, past H.M. Stanley hospital, with the cathedral tower peeping over the trees. The leading coach was one of the 'Coronation' stock that visited America in 1939, which had no corridor connection at the brake end, and which became part of the 'Land Cruise' train stock almost from the start. The station goods shed can be seen in the distance .   *Author's collection*

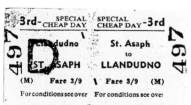

(lower). **St.Asaph. 17th August 1961.** BR Standard Class 4MT 4-6-0 No.**75026** allocated to Machynlleth shed (89C), although in fact outstationed at Pwllheli, pulls away from St.Asaph with a 'Land Cruise' working on the final leg on single track, to Foryd Junction. The cathedral tower is visible over the house tops. For some reason, the trains that originated on the Western Region rarely carried smokebox headboards.
Author's collection

(upper). **St.Asaph. c.1951.** The station stands above the town, and exposed to some degree to the elements. The station building was located on the Up side and was constructed of red brick, faced with local stone surrounds for doors and window frames. Nevertheless there was little protection for the passengers travelling to Rhyl, and even less for passengers to Denbigh, who were required to cross the line by the very exposed footbridge. The shelter on the Down platform was devoid of any heating and partly exposed to the elements. The line crossed the main A55 road immediately north of the station, and the Vale of Clwyd Railway provided a bridge for a single line of track, which meant that the Down loop line commenced by the Up side ramp, causing the platforms to be staggered. Beyond the footbridge was an raised exposed lever frame with protective guard rails, just visible in this view.

L.G.R.P. No.24423

St.Asaph

Located 2 miles 868 yards from Trefnant, St.Asaph was the largest of the intermediate stations on the Vale of Clwyd line. The station buildings were located on the Up side, and contained a Station Master's house within the complex. Originally there was only one platform, but a second was installed on the Down side in 1877. The line ran into the station from Rhuddlan over a single span bridge across the A55, which passed through the town until the 1970's when the by-pass was built. Although provision had been made for double track over the road, only a single width bridge was provided and this inhibited the commencement of the Down side passing loop which in turn necessitated the platforms being staggered. An open front shelter was provided on the Down side and a footbridge was added in 1899. A barrow crossing was located at the Rhuddlan end, and passengers usually used this in preference to using the footbridge. After the loop was lifted, the footbridge was removed, but the shelter survived until after the line was lifted. The main station building survives, now in private ownership.

The goods yard was located at the Denbigh end on the Up side and contained a landing stage, horse landing and a goods shed. There were three sidings, one of which passed through the goods warehouse, whilst another was designated as a coal siding and used by the local Coal Merchants. Facilities listed in *The R.C.H. Handbook of Stations 1929* gave facilities for handling Furniture Vans, Livestock, Horse Boxes and Prize Cattle Vans, Carriages by Passenger Train and 5 ton crane power. In addition to the usual traffic, the yard dealt with timber, engineering equipment, agricultural equipment and produce, chiefly for the Vale of Clwyd Farmers co-operative which had a depot on the site. There was considerable cattle traffic dealt with by the station and some out-going milk traffic in churns, from Llanerch Dairies. The goods warehouse survives at the time of writing.

St.Asaph was a Staff Token Exchange station, the instruments being located in booking office. A ground frame was installed on the Up platform under the footbridge at the Foryd Junction end; the frame held 15 levers of which three were spare, and which controlled the loop points, horse landing points, point lock and signals. According to Goodall (*The Vale of Clwyd Railway. p.49*), the token for the Trefnant section was coloured red and became a miniature token in 1949. The Token for the section to Rhuddlan was coloured blue. The Down loop was removed some time after May 1957, probably about the same time that the loop at Trefnant was lifted. About this time too, the yard capacity was reduced.

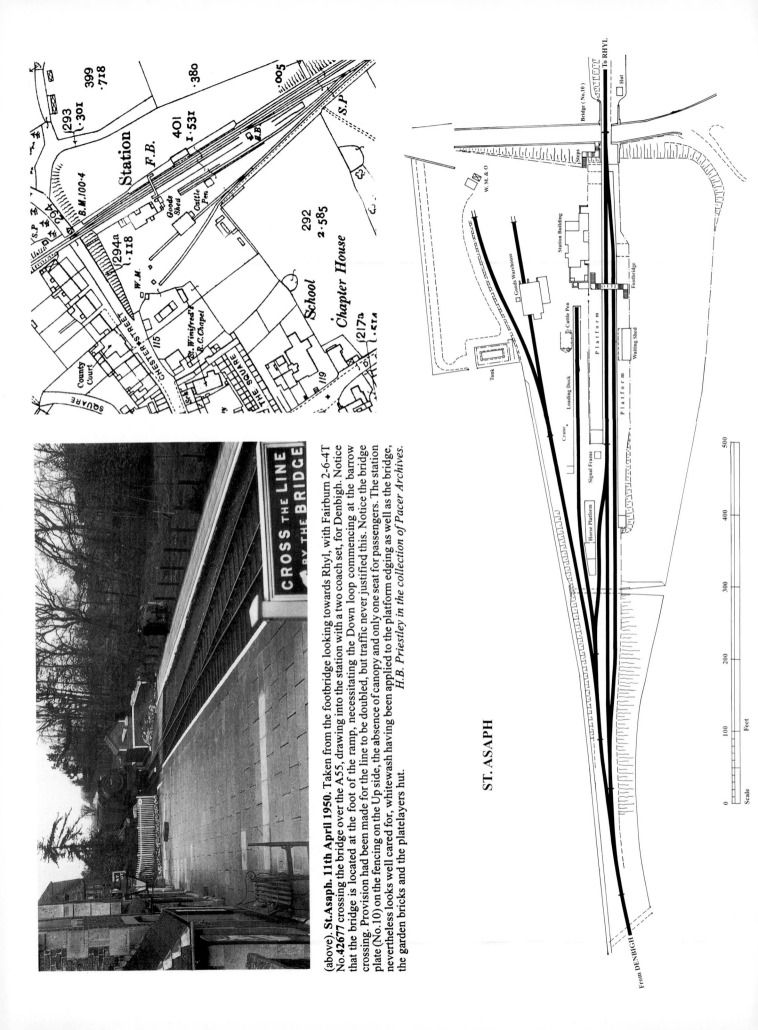

(above). **St.Asaph. 11th April 1950.** Taken from the footbridge looking towards Rhyl, with Fairburn 2-6-4T No.42677 crossing the bridge over the A55, drawing into the station with a two coach set, for Denbigh. Notice that the bridge is located at the foot of the ramp, necessitating the Down loop commencing at the barrow crossing. Provision had been made for the line to be doubled, but traffic never justified this. Notice the bridge plate (No.10) on the fencing on the Up side, the absence of canopy and only one seat for passengers. The station nevertheless looks well cared for, whitewash having been applied to the platform edging as well as the bridge, the garden bricks and the platelayers hut.

H.B. Priestley in the collection of Pacer Archives.

ST. ASAPH

(upper). **St.Asaph. 9th May 1949.** The south end of the Up side platform. The raised lever frame by the footbridge has the frame diagram mounted on posts with indicators enclosed alongside, illuminated by a gas lamp. Notice the lattice signal post for the Up starter.
E.S. Russell.

(centre). **St.Asaph. 18th August 1960.** The Cambrian Radio Cruise, headed by Class 4MT 4-6-0 No.**75054** and its six coach formation passes through the Up platform on the outward journey. Notice that although the Down loop has been removed, the platform and shelter remained intact. *Author's collection*

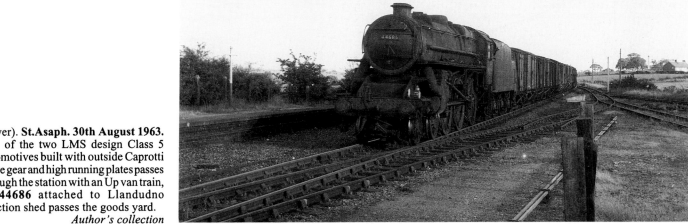

(lower). **St.Asaph. 30th August 1963.** One of the two LMS design Class 5 locomotives built with outside Caprotti valve gear and high running plates passes through the station with an Up van train, No.**44686** attached to Llandudno Junction shed passes the goods yard.
Author's collection

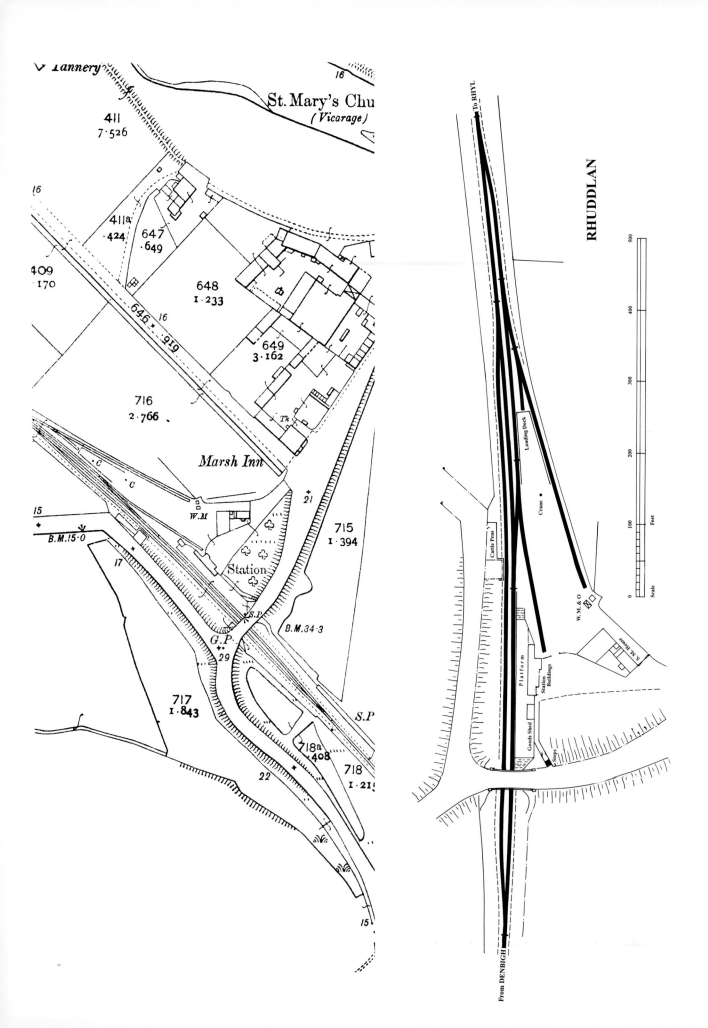

Tannery

St. Mary's Chu
(Vicarage)

411
7·526

16

411a
·424

409
·170

647
·649

648
1·233

646 × ·919
16

716
2·766

649
3·162

Tk

15

B.M.15·0

17

Marsh Inn

W.M

Station

S.P.

21

715
1·394

B.M.34·3

G.P.
29

717
1·843

718a
·408

22

S.P.

718
1·21

15

RHUDDLAN

To RHYL

Loading Dock

Crane

Cattle Pens

W.M. & O

S.M. House

Platform

Station Buildings

Goods Shed

Steps

From DENBIGH

500

400

300

200

100

Feet

Scale

0

Rhuddlan. n.d. The station was located on the Down side, and was a staff token station, although two passenger trains were not allowed to cross here. The Up loop was added after the station opened, and was used exclusively by goods trains. There seems to be an unusually large collection of parcels awaiting handling, with two sets of milk churns on either side of the main building. The goods yard has an interesting collection of wagons including two private owner vehicles, one of which is identified as belonging to Barton & Co. Behind them is a quantity of timber being loaded by the yard crane. Perhaps the staff are having a rest from handling all the small parcels consignments!   *D. Thompson*

Rhuddlan

2 miles 907 yards from St.Asaph, 2 miles 423 yards from Foryd Junction, Rhuddlan station was located on the edge of this historic village, in sight of the famous castle. The station was on the Down side, and consisted of a single platform with a brick built building, perhaps the very steep pitch of the roof being its most noticeable feature. The Station Master's house was detached from the main building. There was a small goods yard on the Down side at the Foryd Junction end of the line which contained two sidings, the larger one having a capacity for 14 wagons, and which was used for loading timber for many years. After the Second World War it was used for Camping Coaches during the season. The shorter siding behind the platform held 9 wagons and was used by the local coal merchants. The station was a Staff Token Exchange point with Foryd Junction and St.Asaph. The instruments were located in the Station Office. There was a loop provided on the Up side, but passenger trains were not allowed to cross at the station. Another loop was provided in the goods yard. A cattle pen was located on the Up side crossing loop. A small ground frame was mounted on the platform at the Foryd Junction end controlling signals. The loop and other points were controlled by individual two lever ground frames using Annett's keys.

The facilities listed in the *R.C.H. Handbook of Stations* specify the same as for St.Asaph, with a yard crane of 5 ton capacity. It is understood that there was at least one other yard crane.

Passenger traffic after World War 1 was always light, as the station was on the edge of Rhuddlan, and involved a somewhat lengthy walk, including a steep hill. When buses started to become commonplace, they passed through the centre of Rhuddlan, and the traffic lost was never regained. There was a slight upsurge during the Second World War, but this declined once an easing of petrol and diesel rationing came about. Freight traffic was significant until the general decline in rail traffic in the late 1950's.

The station site and buildings were cleared to make way for a road traffic roundabout and there is no trace beyond stretches of the overgrown trackbed.

(upper). **Rhuddlan. 1956.** Although the Down Starter is pulled 'off', an unidentified Ivatt Class 2MT 2-6-0 pauses at the platform whilst working Light Engine from Rhyl to Denbigh. Wagons stand on the Up Goods loop, but were not part of a train. Just visible is the small lever frame that controlled signals.   *G.H. Platt*

(centre left). **Rhuddlan. 1956.** Taken from the road overbridge looking towards Foryd Junction. The goods yard is still in use, but mainly by the local coal merchant. The former timber siding was used to house camping coaches, and at one time as many as four being located there.   *G.H. Platt*

(centre right). **Rhuddlan. n.d.** Taken from the road overbridge looking towards Denbigh. As the station was only open for a few hours each day for freight traffic, it was normally unmanned, and the Up home signal was left in the 'off' position.
                    The late Ivor Vaughan

(lower). **Rhuddlan. 27th August 1954.** An afternoon train for Denbigh pauses at Rhuddlan station, but no passengers board or alight. Notice the small eight lever ground frame by the gentleman's toilets, which only controlled signals.
The late H.C. Casserley

(upper). **Foryd Junction. n.d.** At one time a station existed at Foryd Junction on the Vale of Clwyd line, but this closed in 1885, replaced by a new station on the Chester & Holyhead main line. The station buildings and the earthworks for the platform remained until the line closed, although the platform earthwork had disappeared some time before then. The main line to St.Asaph is on the right, the lines on the left hand side provided a run round loop facility without occupying the running line, for traffic off the Foryd Pier line.

L.G.R.P. No.5410

(lower). **Foryd Junction. 31st October 1957.** Foryd Junction signalbox, taken in the six foot between the Down Fast and Slow lines, looking towards Rhyl. The Vale of Clwyd line passes behind the box and can be seen on the right of the picture. A 2-arm signal on the branch protects the main line, whilst in the distance, the junction signals for the Down line can be seen. In the foreground, the plates for the bridge over the Foryd Pier line glisten in the wet weather. A look-out flagman stands facing the traffic, presumably to protect the photographer. *British Railways London Midland Region.*

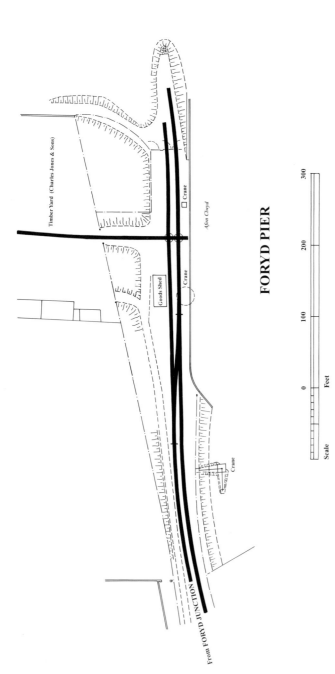

FORYD PIER

Timber Yard (Charles Jones & Sons)

Crane

Crane

Goods Shed

Afon Clwyd

Crane

From FORYD JUNCTION

Scale — Feet

0   100   200   300

(left). **Foryd Pier. 31st October 1957.** Another look at the Chester & Holyhead main line passing over the Foryd Pier branch, this time looking north towards the estuary. Despite the poor condition of track, trains still worked to Foryd Harbour, on the west bank of the river where a timber merchant regularly received supplies. A train worked Mondays to Fridays to the harbour, usually worked by the Rhyl station pilot. It is not certain whether the two spans were in anticipation of doubling the line, or whether the right hand bridge traversed a footpath.
British Railways London Midland Region.

(right). **Foryd Junction. 31st October 1957.** The Chester & Holyhead main line passed over the Foryd Pier line just west of the junction with the Vale of Clwyd line. Originally constructed as a private tramway, nevertheless it survived as a freight only line until 6th April 1959. Beyond the bridge can be seen coaches stored on the sidings adjoining the Vale of Clwyd main line.
British Railways London Midland Region

(upper). **Foryd Pier Line. 1956.** From Foryd Junction the branch was single track up to the point where it crossed the Rhyl to Abergele road. It was at this point that the promoters intended to establish their passenger station, and the track was doubled to provide the necessary run round facilities. In the event, passenger services never worked over the line, and it remained a freight branch throughout its existence. The line crossed the road on the level, and hand operated gates, were installed, protected by signals on either side of the crossing.   *G.H. Platt*

(lower). **Foryd Harbour. 1956.** It had been intended that Vale of Clwyd trains would work to Foryd Harbour, where they would connect with ships bound for Liverpool, and this harbour was developed to accommodate the vessels. The scheme came to naught, and the line became a rural freight only branch line, serving the timber yard and other occasional traffic. Traffic was generally light, consisting mainly of a few open wagons or the occasional van. A goods shed was provided, seen here, but generally the facilities were under-used.   *G.H. Platt*

Foryd Junction. 31st October 1957. Another look at the junction, this time taken from the Up side, looking towards Rhyl. The bridge over the Foryd Pier line is in the foreground. The gantry over the Slow and Fast lines relate to protecting the junction, whilst the centre arm relates to the crossover from Fast to Slow lines, used mainly by trains off the branch which threaded over the Down lines then gained the Down Slow for the final stage into Rhyl. Beyond the gantry, the line crosses the river Clwyd, then skirts Marine Lake, which provided standard gauge travellers with a glimpse of the 15" gauge Marine Lake Railway which ran parallel for about a quarter of a mile.

British Railways London Midland Region.

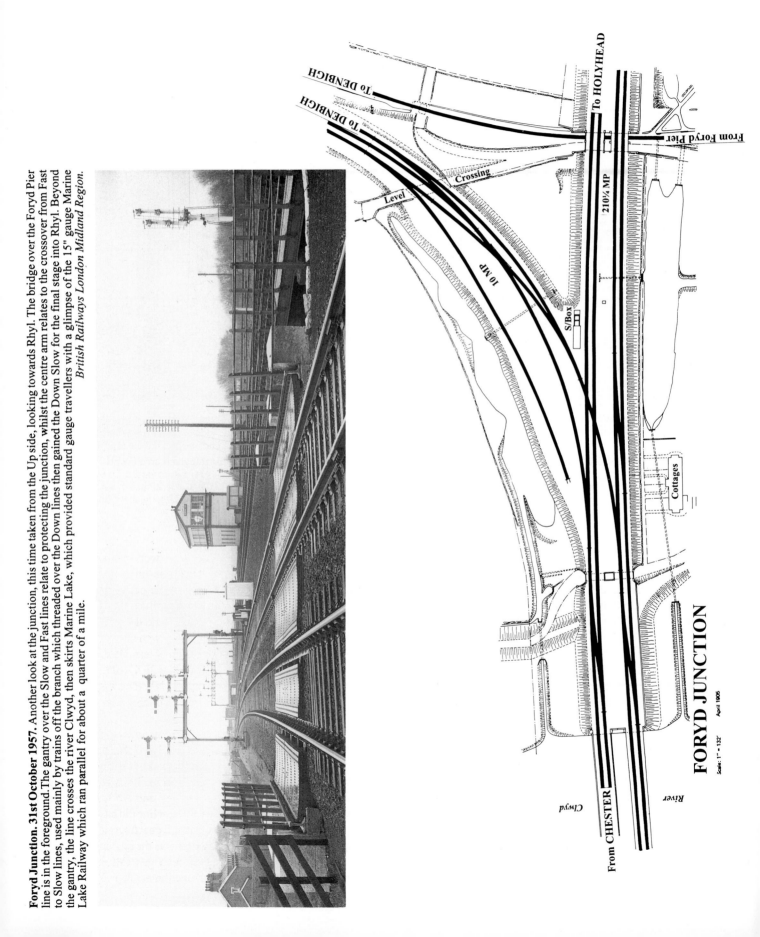

FORYD JUNCTION

Scale: 1" = 132'   April 1905

To DENBIGH

To DENBIGH

To HOLYHEAD

From Foryd Pier

Level

Crossing

210¼ MP

10 MP

S/Box

Cottages

River

Clwyd

From CHESTER

Rhyl. 1950's. LMS Class 5 4-6-0 No.**45419** of Walsall (3C) shed, after working an excursion train from the Birmingham area (W713) to Rhyl, after passengers had all departed, drew out of the Down Loop platform onto the Down Slow line, and set back through the Down side yard to the carriage sidings where the stock would be serviced prior to the return working. On the extreme left is Rhyl shed, with the smokebox of a class 2P just visible. It is possible that this was a mid-week working, as most empty stock trains were worked forward to Llandudno Junction to avoid blocking the main lines. Frequently trains were signalled from block to block, such was the congestion. *K. Field.*

Rhyl

Most but not all passenger trains for the Vale of Clwyd line departed from or terminated at the bay platform on the Down side, which had a scissors crossover near the stops enabling locomotives to be released. Access for Up trains to the bay was off the Up Fast line. The main platforms at Rhyl were over 1000ft in length, primarily to accommodate the lengthy holiday traffic trains. Nevertheless the Denbigh bay platforms on the Down side were in excess of 500ft in length, and even allowing for the fact that using the scissors crossover to release an incoming locomotive would shorten the available platform space, there was sufficient room to cater for all the Vale of Clwyd line's needs. In 1954 the Llandudno Land Cruise train worked into one of the two bay platforms. The locomotive that worked the train, usually one of Bangor's 2-6-4T, drew right up to the buffer stops. The Class 2 locomotive working forward came off shed, and set back onto the stock, which meant that there were two locomotives and six coaches, all at the platform face. Once the Land Cruise pulled away, the other locomotive was released to go on shed.

In the summer of 1939 Rhyl shed worked the first train of the day with a pull-push 'motor' train to Denbigh and return which then worked back to Denbigh then to Mold and return. The working

timetable does not show the motor train working as such back to Rhyl, so presumably it worked back as an ordinary working. Otherwise most trains were worked in the conventional manner, locomotives running around the stock for the return journey at the destination. Some workings from Rhyl worked through to Ruthin at this time, and two worked through to Corwen on weekdays, (three on Wednesdays and Saturdays), but most terminated at Denbigh. Some workings were in the hands of Class 2P 4-4-0 tender engines, but most at this time were worked by ex LNWR tank engines. Stock was normally two non-corridor coaches, which rarely deviated from the line.

Various theories have been put forward as to why there were no through coach workings off the Vale of Clwyd. The most plausible reason seems to be that passenger traffic was purely local, and there was so little demand that cross platform facilities were adequate. The same was true of the Conwy valley and Amlwch branches, whereas the Afonwen-Caernarfon-Bangor line did have demand for sufficient numbers to justify the through coach working, or rather through stock working. Another factor was the fact that passengers wishing to travel to Chester and beyond generally used the line through Mold and effected the connection at Chester.

(upper). **Rhyl. 1930's.** This pre-war view of Rhyl from the air shows the grid pattern of the town, with the railway running from top to bottom of the right hand side of the picture, and unfortunately not very distinct. In the foreground is Marine Lake, and the track of the 15" gauge miniature railway that encircled the lake can clearly be seen.   *V.R. Anderson collection*

(lower). **Rhyl. June 1932.** Holiday crowds wait on the Up platform at Rhyl, which was little changed from LNWR days. In the distance, a train for Denbigh waits in the bay platform, partly concealed by the canopy supports. Rhyl was disadvantaged by only having one through Up platform road, which caused severe congestion on summer Saturdays, particularly in the immediate post war period.   *V.R. Anderson collection*

Rhyl. July 1957. Rhyl shed yard, with Ivatt 2-6-2T No.**41276** and Standard Class 4MT 4-6-0 No.**75033** awaiting their next turn of duty. The tank engines were used on "The Welsh Dragon" which operated a shuttle service between Rhyl and Llandudno, and was, as far as is known, the only steam operated pull-push named train working in the U.K. The Class 4 locomotives were used on the 'Land Cruise' trains and this was their first season on these duties. Previously they had been worked by Ivatt Class 2MT 2-6-0 engines. Beyond the tank engine is the mechanised coal plant - Rhyl version, which was an improvement on what had gone before. In the distance is the 60ft turntable, wedged between the shed wall and the boundary fence.   *W.G. Rear*

Motive Power.

Whilst traffic working over the line centred on Denbigh shed, there is some confusion about the origins of the shed, and which, unfortunately, nothing new has surfaced the clarify the situation. What was written in the companion work in this series applies equally to traffic working over the DR&C and the VofC lines. Consequently most of this section concentrates on the workings of Rhyl shed. In the brief period prior to the LNWR assuming control on the line, it is likely that one locomotive sufficed, and probably only one driver, fireman and cleaner, based at Gwyddelwern until the line extended to the temporary station at Corwen. When the final connection with the Llangollen & Corwen Railway was made, it was natural to transfer the facilities. In fact it would appear that the loco shed at Gwyddelwern straddled the running line, and permission to extend operations was conditional on the removal of the shed! Corwen was always an outstation, and the Loco Department established a presence from the commencement of services. Initially this probably amounted to no more than the locomotive and staff from Gwyddelwern, and probably remained the same until Ruthin Loco closed, when the work was shared between Denbigh and Corwen. It is likely that two locomotives and between two and four sets of men, plus a fitter and cleaners to attend to routine maintenance comprised the LNWR presence in the town. Facilities were provided by and shared with the GWR. The GWR decision to close the depot and move some of the staff and locos to Bala in 1927 inhibited the LMS operation, the latter company declined the GWR offer to take over the depot, transferring its staff to Denbigh. The shed was demolished at some unspecified date in the 1930's, but the

track, inspection pit and turntable survived for many years. The water tanks remained in use until the line closed to all traffic in 1964. Denbigh shed was never considered of sufficient importance to be an independent unit and at first came under Chester until April 1899 when it was "transferred" to Llandudno Junction, which become independent of Bangor and given the shed code '38' by the LNWR. Denbigh was coded 38D and it is understood that locomotives attached to the shed carried enamel 38D plates.

The depot compliment of locomotives and staff was at its peak in the latter years of the LNWR, but by the time the LMS came into being, traffic was already on the decline and work gradually filtered away mainly to road transport. Under the reorganisation of the Motive Power structure, with the establishment of the Concentration and Garage Depot Schemes in 1935, Denbigh became a sub-shed of Rhyl (7D) which had, up until this time, itself been a sub-shed to Llandudno Junction.

J.M. Dunn, as Foreman Fitter at Llandudno Junction was asked by his superior, Mr J.T. King, to visit Denbigh shed and report on its facilities. His report, dated 3rd February 1938, makes interesting reading, and is reproduced in full here:

Sir,

Denbigh Shed
As desired, I give below a report on my visit to Denbigh Shed today.
Engine Records
The Wash-out Cards were not available for inspection as they had been sent to Llandudno Junction in accordance with the daily practice.

The Examination Cards and Boiler Sheets were inspected and found to be correctly entered up to date.

A copy of the Llandudno Junction X-day Repair Card was given to Mr Stevens and he was advised to obtain a hectograph pad with a view to preparing a similar card for use at Denbigh.

Standard Examinations

*A certain amount of confusion seems to exist with regard to the Standard Examination Instructions and it is suggested that the Denbigh copies of the circulars concerned be sent to Llandudno Junction for revision. Copies of the Standard Examinations and Experimental Fittings Circulars are **not** posted in the shed and are **not** accessible to the R.E. Staff at all hours. A suitable desk should be provided for the R.E. Staff.*

Notice Cases

The glasses of two of the notice cases were broken and these are being ordered. The cases are at present placed over the fitter's bench which is not a suitable position and it is suggested that a better one be found.

A number of notices in one of the cases were pinned one over the other and they presented a very untidy appearance.

Fitters' Bench and Tools

The fitters bench is in a deplorable condition and together with the two vices fixed to it, requires renewal. There are, at present, cupboards under the bench which form a general rubbish-dump and these should be replaced by a shadow-board for the tools.

The buffer-plank trolley is, at the moment, being used as staging in connection with coal-stacking and it is suggested that this is not a desirable use for it.

A large number of surplus and damaged tools were collected and some of these will require to be replaced. A quantity of scrap brass-work was also found and instructions were given for all this material to be sent to Llandudno Junction for attention.

The small tools, such as stocks and dies etc., were in very poor condition and although the Denbigh user might not warrant the supply of new ones, perhaps second-hand ones might be sent from Llandudno Junction and the old ones from Denbigh sent for repairs.

The fitters cupboards are of the old fashioned type and it is suggested that a standard nest of cupboards be supplied.

Sand Furnace

With regard to the demolition of the sand-furnace, Fitter Ewer said that he had no mate and was unable to obtain any assistance as all the cleaners were working on the coal-stack. He was also short of tools for the job and these will be sent as soon as possible.

Stores

There are a number of old-fashioned pigeon-holes which might be replaced by a small standard stores rack with advantage. Mr Stevens said that the oil tanks in the Stores were not used and perhaps the question of their removal might be considered. He also said that he had been unable to obtain shafts for big hammers and cleaning fluid for the lavatory pans from Llandudno Junction stores.

I am, sir, etc.

A handwritten note was appended to this letter as follows:

"When I handed this report to Mr King he did not bother to look at it but put it straight into a drawer. He never referred to it except to tell me a few weeks later, that he did not wish me to go to Denbigh again. JMD"

It is reported that the locomotive strength at Denbigh during the early 1920's amounted to 20 locomotives, and probably in excess of thirty sets of traincrew. This had dwindled to eleven locomotives by 1937. Prior to the Second World War, most of the locomotives at Denbigh comprised ex LNWR tank engines, an LMS Standard Class 2 4-4-0 and a Standard Class 3F 0-6-0. but for statistical purposes, grouped with the Rhyl allocation. As can be determined from J.M.Dunn's account, only running repairs were undertaken,

together with routine boiler wash-out. "X" examinations were conducted at Rhyl, and the diagramming of the locomotives would have ensured that the specific loco was at Rhyl on the appointed day. Replacements would have been provided by Rhyl or Llandudno Junction.

J.M. Dunn gives the allocation at Denbigh in January 1948 as follows:

LMS 2 Cyl 4-4-0 Class 2P: 629, 646.

LNWR 2-4-2T Class 1PT: 6632, 6658, 6687, 6691, 6701, 6712

Midland R. 0-6-0 Class 3F: 3396

This dwindled further by summer 1952 to seven locomotives. The six ex LNWR 2-4-2T had been replaced by four modern Ivatt Class 2P 2-6-2T. According to Vernon Roberts, currently driving at Chester, there were fourteen rostered turns booked to the depot at the time of closure on 19th September 1955.

RHYL SHED

For many years Rhyl was a sub-shed to Llandudno Junction in LNWR and early LMS days, coded 38R. With the Motive Power reorganisation, it became a Garage Depot in its own right, and was accordingly designated as 7D, under Llandudno Junction Concentration Depot and district, listed at 7A. When the district was combined with Chester in May 1952, the coding for Rhyl shed was changed to "6K", which it retained until closure on 11th February 1963. The complete closure of the Chester-Mold-Denbigh line and withdrawal of all but limited mail, parcels and freight traffic to Ruthin, along the Vale of Clwyd line, coupled with the closure of the smaller stations on the North Wales Coast and replacement of steam with diesel traction effectively removed the need for locomotive facilities.

The shed stood on the Up side of the track at the Llandudno Junction end of the station, hemmed in between the main line and Kinmel Street West. It comprised a three-road brick built structure, and was enlarged on more than one occasion, and re-roofed about 1938. About this time a vacuum operated 60ft turntable was installed, replacing a smaller hand-operated table on approximately the same site. A water tank supplied the Motive Power Depot, and a column on the Down Slow line.

Most of the work covered by Rhyl shed was local, which was reflected in the allocation of locomotives. On 1st January 1948, the depot was host to the following:

Midland Class 2P 4-4-0	396, 494.
LMS Class 2P 4-4-0	658
LNWR 2-4-2T Class 1PT	6727
LNWR 0-6-0 18" Goods Class 2F	28335, 28616
L&Y 0-6-0 Class 3F	12116, 12125, 12167, 12338, 12356
LNWR 0-6-2T Class 2FT	27562, 27585, 27627.

The variety of locomotives allocated to the shed since Nationalisation has been extensive, and set out below is a comprehensive list of its residents, kindly supplied by Richard Strange, of Steam Archive Services, taken from the Official Transfer Sheets:

40001, 40060, 40084, 40097, 40101, 40105, 40118, 40126, 41043, 40324, 40377, 40396, 40420, 40430, 40433, 494, 40495, 40515, 40529, 40580, 40589, 40628, 40629, 40646, 40671, 40675, 40679, 41210, 41211, 41216, 41224, 41226, 41230, 41231, 41233, 41244, 41276, 41277, 41285, 41287, 41320, 41321, 41324, 43378, 43396, 43618, 43981, 44348, 44367, 46420,

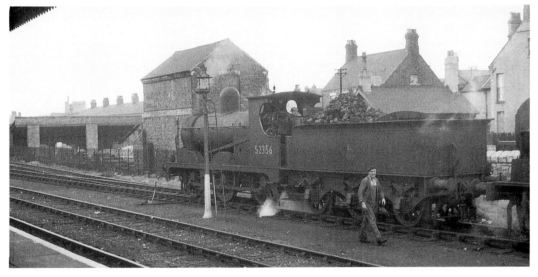

(upper). **Rhyl Shed. c.1958.** An unusual view taken from inside Rhyl shed, looking towards the station. LMS Standard Class 3F 0-6-0T No.**47350** stands on the turntable road, presumably booked to shed shunting duties. Alongside Ivatt 2-6-2T No.**41276** seemingly out of steam. Further up the yard is an unidentified ex L&Y 0-6-0. Another loco is shunting stock by the bay platform. Rhyl No.2 signal box towers above the tracks at the end of No.1 platform. *Huw Edwards*

(centre). **Rhyl. 1952.** Ex L&Y 0-6-0 No.**52356** on the shed shunt moves another locomotive about the yard. Many of these 0-6-0 locomotives were transferred from the Central Division to replace ageing LNW engines at Rhyl and Bangor. They were regarded as good pullers, but enthusiasm for them was tempered by temperamental injectors, which required cold water baths at times; the screw reverse, which was not ideally suited for shunting operations, and the exposed cab, which was not conducive to tender first working. *Gordon Coltas.*

(lower). **Rhyl. 1952.** Rhyl was frequently the repository for locomotives working their final days to acquire the necessary mileage prior to shopping, or more frequently for scrapping. Here, four years after nationalisation, a 'Cauliflower' believed to be No.**58053** but whose number is not visible, and Class 1P No.**46643**, both still carrying L.M.S. on the tender and tank sides, get moved about the shed yard by 2-6-2T No.**41231**. *Gordon Coltas*

46422, 46423, 46424, 46425, 46426, 46428, 46430, 46432, 46433, 46434, 46445, 46448, 6632, 46643, 6658, 46687, 6691, 46701, 46712, 46727, 47350, 47507, 47669, 10665, 10667, 10670, 50675, 50687, 50695, 10696, 52107, 52119, 52125, 52162, 52167, 52172, 52233, 52338, 52356, 52432, 52438, 52453, 52608, 52619, 58287, 58293, 58362, 58364, 28392, 58392 (28505), 28521, 28529, 28580, 28585, 28589, 58427 (28616), 27562, 27585, 58888 (27602), 58889 (27603), 58893 (27627), 27669, 58903 (7711), 58911 (7746), 7765, 58921 (7782), 58924 (7791), 7822, 75028, 75031, 75033, 75034, 75035, 75051, 75053, 75054, 78017, 78031, 78032, 78033, 78034, 78035, 78038, 78039, 78055, 78056, 78057, 84003.

The combined Rhyl and Denbigh allocations after Nationalisation peaked in 1951 when 26 locomotives were allocated to the parent shed on the first Saturday of each year, with the ex L&Y 0-6-0 contingent of seven members providing the largest group. The following year saw this number reduced to 21 locos, although this climbed back to 25 for 1955. The following year saw this reduced by nine, and the numbers diminished until the closure in 1963, when three LMS Class 3F 0-6-0T Nos 47350, 47507 and 47669 and BR Standard Class 2MT 2-6-2T No.84003 booked off the shed for the last time, the first two 'Jinties' moving to Mold Junction, the other two transferring to Llandudno Junction.

It should be noted that each Shed on the London Midland Region of British Railways had a block of Diagrams allocated to them, which were sub-divided into two sections - Passenger Engine Workings and Freight Engine Workings, each with three categories, which tend to confuse the unsuspecting. The individual arrangements sheets were cross-referenced.

Engine Workings:

These defined what work the engines themselves did. The traincrews involved were identified on the right-hand side of the working against the trip. This could involve different crew turns, and from different depots on different days of the week. e.g. Rhyl Turn 60.

Engine and Men's Workings

This category was used when engine and men from the same depot followed the work pattern for part or the whole of the shift, although the engine might subsequently be worked by other crews. e.g. Rhyl Turn 2.

Enginemen's Workings.

This category specified what each set of men did for their shift. This would also indicate what the Engine Turn number was, and which shed provided it. e.g. Rhyl Turn 38.

At many sheds, the Enginemen's work was grouped in Links, which could vary from a single turn to a link of any size, according to a variety of factors, such as routes, seniority, class of work etc. At Denbigh, being one of the smaller sheds on the Western Division, and apart from one or two specialised duties, the men worked 'round the board', covering all the Turns in rotation, but not necessarily in chronological order and not necessarily the same turn every day. It is understood that until Rhyl shed was given its own code (7D) men worked every duty in rotation. After that date, a link structure was established. Latterly this consisted of the Top Link of 8 Passenger Turns; No.2. Link comprised 12 Passenger Turns; No.3 Link had 8 Turns and work was a mixture of Passenger and Freight work; No.4 Link had 8 Freight Turns; No.5 Link consisted of 2 Turns, working the Early and Late Rhyl Yard Shunt and No.6. Link worked the Early and Late Turning Duties on the Shed Yard, usually worked by men who had medical problems, and were confined to the yard. At

one time there was a Motor Train Link, which covered the Holywell Town Passenger Turns (Earlies and Lates), and *The Welsh Dragon,* although it is possible that these were incorporated into the Top Link after W.W.II. Whilst the Enginemen's Turns listed below are perhaps untypical of the work previously undertaken by Rhyl men in the period up until 1960, they give an insight into the complexity of Engine and Men's Diagramming. At this period in time, (late 1961), the number of Engines actually based at Rhyl had been reduced to four (see Locomotive Turns earlier) and much of the work that involved Rhyl men working on Chester or Mold Junction engines would, twelve months earlier, have been done on Rhyl based engines. Frequently the men were required to take up their workings away from the depot, which involved travelling time, and actual contact time on the footplate was much reduced. Nevertheless it is interesting to note that 21 sets of men were required to complete the scheduled work 'on the road', and in all probability, at least another three sets would be required for Shed Turning duties. The chart below indicates the normal daily requirements.

Details of Rhyl shed working in LNWR and LMS days are very sketchy, relying almost entirely on personal recollections, which unfortunately have to be regarded with caution, until corroborated or proved by documentary evidence. According to Percy Harrison, who was the LDC Chairman for many years, interviewed in 1984, there were fourteen sets of men based at the shed during World War I, and work consisted mainly of local passenger working to Chester or Llandudno Junction, Denbigh, Chester via Denbigh, Holywell Town and Dyserth branches. Freight work seemed to consist of the daily freight to Denbigh and Foryd Pier, as well as the Abergele trip and Holywell Junction shunt. During 1918/19 two passed firemen worked daily (one on Sundays) as pilotmen for Military trains working to Kinmel Park Camp, from Foryd Junction to Rhyl station and return. There was some increase in local work after 1930, when work was transferred from Denbigh to Rhyl, and men learnt the road to Bangor, Birkenhead, Manchester Exchange and Crewe, mainly for summer season traffic. It would seem that twenty eight sets of men were required on Saturdays for main line passenger work alone during the summer of 1939, although this figure is not supported by any documentary proof. Rhyl shed men worked *The Welsh Dragon,* an innovation that caught the public imagination, running several times a day during the season between Rhyl and Llandudno. It was a three coach Pull-Push working, complete with Headboard for locomotive and Motor Driving Coach, and extremely popular with the holidaymakers. The Land Cruise trains were additional workings to the Rosters. The 'Motor Train Link' catered for the former, but the Land Cruise trains were worked at one time by a special seasonal link staffed by Passed Firemen who learnt the Road' throughout and in both directions. On the occasions I worked the circuit, Frank Beech was the driver and understand that this was his preserve for the most summer seasons. Latterly the Land Cruise work was placed in No.2. Link. However, the Rhyl to Aberdovey via Caernarfon Turn along the Cambrian Coast was worked exclusively by Bangor men.

According to George Sheedy, Vic. Thomas and Gus Williams, Rhyl shed passed firemen were almost guaranteed driving turns on summer Saturdays, and consequently local men were somewhat reluctant to move to other depots in a bid for promotion.

(upper). **Rhyl M.P.D. 1958.** LMS Standard Class 3F 0-6-0T No.**47350** moves off the turntable road heading for the yard throat. It will then set back to the shed disc and cross the main line to the Down side where it will work as required in the goods yard or the carriage sidings. *Huw Edwards*

(left). **Rhyl M.P.D. June 1947.**Shed master at this time was John Robinson, grandson of Ben Robinson, who drove LNWR loco No.**790** *Hardwicke* between Crewe and Carlisle in the 1896 period commonly referred to as the 'Railway Race to the North'. He was a much loved boss, and still regarded wit affection by all who knew him, both at Rhyl and at Mold Junction. *courtesy Anthony Robinson.*

(right). **Rhyl M.P.D. November 1947.** Shed staff pose for a group photograph.Back row, left to right are T. Williams, F. Tasker, T. Austin, Bill Neal (Engineering Department); Middle Row: Percy Harrison, John Robinson (Running Shed Foreman), J. Pasonage, J. McDonald, Lew Jones, Harry Boulter, Bob Jones, Percy Jones; Front Row: ?. Maddox, T. Hornby, Jack Passey and T. Molloy. *courtesy Anthony Robinson.*

The implications for Rhyl men with the withdrawal of passenger services between Chester, Denbigh and Ruthin, and complete closure of the line between Hendre Lime Sidings and Denbigh and between Ruthin and Corwen were profound whilst other sheds affected by the line closures were:

Chester Loco Turns: 8A, 8B, 9, 28A, 28B, 29, 30, 35, 36, 39, 685

Chester Men's Turns: 72, 73, 74, 98, 154, 160, 228, 230, 240, 241, 242, 243, 244, 246, 247, 252, 253, 258, 319, 320, 321, 324, 635, 636, 656, 681, 687, 690, 893 and 917.

Mold Junction Loco Turns: 10A, 10B, 10C, 100, 105, 111, 122A, 122B, 124A, 126A, 126B, 133,

Mold Junction Men's Turns: 24, 40, 232, 244, 245, 250, 251, 252, 253, 255, 256, 258, 259, 260, 320, 330, 415 and 433.

Llandudno Junction Loco Turns. 3A and 3B.

Llandudno Junction. Men's Turns. 121, 125, 130, 132 and 268.

Crewe North Men's Turns. 718 and 729.

Holyhead Loco Turns. 3A, 3B and 3C.

Warrington Loco Turns. 5A, 5B and 5C.

Warrington Men's Turns. 653.

Willesden Loco Turn. 38A, 38B.

Birkenhead Loco Turn. 83.

Birkenhead Men's Turns. 83, 155, 182, 349 and 422.

Edge Hill Loco Turn. 701A, 701B and 701C.

Edge Hill Men's Turn 1006.

Rhyl M.P.D. naturally was the most affected, and it is worthwhile looking at some of the weekly roster of booked turns prior to closure.

LOCOMOTIVE TURNS
(as at September 1961).

Mon	Tue	Wed	Thu	Fri	Sat	Sun
2	2	2	2	2	4	
19	19	19	19	19	20	
60	60	60	60	60		
72	72	72	72	72	74	

Turn 2/4	Ex LMS Class 2 2-6-0	
Turn 19/20	Ex LMS Class 2 2-6-2T	
Turn 60	Ex Mid Class 3F 0-6-0	
Turn 72/4	Ex L&Y Class 3 0-6-0	

RHYL ENGINEMEN'S TURNS
(as at September 1961)

	Mon	Tue	Wed	Thu	Fri	Sat	Sun
	2	2	2	2	2		
	3	3	3	3	3		
						4	
						17	
	19	19	19	19	19		
						20	
	25	25	25	25	25		
	26	26	26	26	26		
						27	
	28	28	28	28	28		
						29	
	30	30	30	30	30		
						31	
						33	
	34	34	34	34	34		
	35	35	35	35	35	35	
		37	37	37	37	37	
	38	38	38	38	38		
						39	
						40	
							42
							43
							44
	46	46	46	46	46		
						47	
						48	
	50	50	50	50	50		
	51	51	51	51	51	51	
				61			
	72	72	72	72	72		
	73	73	73	73	73		
	74	74	74	74	74	74	
						75	
	82	82	82	82	82		
		84	84	84	84		
	85	85	85	85	85	85	
						87	
	88	88	88	88	88		
						89	
						97	
Daily Turns	19	21	21	22	21	20	3

RHYL
Turn 4

ENGINE WORKING ONLY

	Rhyl M. P. D.	6.00am LE	SO	(87)
6.30am	Denbigh			
6.30	SHUNT (FRT)	8.05	SO	
	Denbigh	8.10 Frt	SO	
8.30	Ruthin		SO	
8.30	SHUNT (FRT)	10.20	SO	
	Ruthin	10.25 Frt	SO	
10.40	Denbigh	11.55 ECS	SO	(27)
12.25pm	Mold	12.55pm.Pass	SO	
1.32	Denbigh	2.10 Pass	SO	(31)
2.24	Ruthin	3.00 Pass	SO	
4.37	Chester	4.50 LE	SO	
4.59	Mold Junction M.P.D.			
	COAL			
	Mold Junction M.P.D.	5.51 LE	SO	
6.00	Chester	6.05 Pass	SO	
8.09	Ruthin	8.25 Pass	SO	
8.39	Denbigh	8.45 ECS	SO	
9.07	Rhyl			

RHYL Turn 2

ENGINE AND MEN'S WORKINGS
ONE CLASS 2 (Ex L.M.S. 2-6-0)

		Book On a.m	Book Off a.m	H. M.	
		7.15	2.16	7 01	
		7.00 S.H.			
	Rhyl M. P. D.	7.45am S.H.	LE	SX	
		8.00am LE	SX		
-	Rhyl	8.30	Pass	SX	
9.36am	Chester				
10.00	SHUNT (PASS)	12.00nn			
	Chester	12.45pm	Pass	SX	
1.46pm	Rhyl	-	LE	SX	
2.01	Rhyl M. P. D.				

RHYL Turn 3

		Book On p.m.	Book Off p.m.	H. M.
		2. 45	10.45	8. 00
	ENGINE PREPARED by Turn 80		SX}	
	Rhyl M. P. D.	3.00pm LE	SX}	
	Rhyl		}	
	RELIEF 3.25pm for 3.30pm Cpld. Chester by Turn 25		SX}	
	PREPARE FRESH ENGINE			
	Rhyl M. P. D.	4.20pm LE	SX	
4.45pm	Denbigh	5.00	Pass	SX
5.14	Ruthin	5.31	Pass	SX
7.04	Chester	8.35	Pass	SX
9.53	Denbigh	10.05	LE	SX
10.30	Rhyl M. P. D.			

RHYL Turn 19

		Book On a.m.	Book Off a.m.	H. M.
		4.00	11.55	7. 55
		3.55 S.H.		

ONE CLASS 2 TANK (Ex L.M.S. 2-6-2) V.C.
PREPARE ENGINE FOR:

		TURN	LEAVES M.P.D.
5.15am Cpld Frt.		28	4.45am "S" SX
6.00am Frt. Shunt		72	5.55am "S" MO
8.00am Denbigh		88	7.30am "L" SX
Pass Shunt		51	8.40am "S" MSX

	Rhyl M.P.D.	7.10am S.H.	LE	SX
		7.25	LE	SX
	Rhyl	7.55	Motor	SX
8.50am	Chester	10.20	Motor	SX
11.25	Rhyl	-	LE	SX
11.40	Rhyl M.P.D.			

RHYL Turn 20

		Book On a. m.	Book Off p. m.	H. M.
		7. 15	2. 16	7. 01
		7. 00 S.H.		

ONE CLASS 2 TANK (Ex L.M.S. 2-6-2) V. C.

	Rhyl M.P.D.	7.45am S.H.LE	SO	
		8.00am LE	SO	
-	Rhyl	8.30	Pass	SO
9.36	Chester			
10.00	SHUNT (PASS)	12.00	SO	
	Chester	12.45pm Pass	SO	
1.46pm	Rhyl	-	LE	SO
2.01	Rhyl M.P.D.			

RHYL Turn 26

		Book On a.m.	Book Off p.m.	H. M.	
		10.40	6.45	8.05	
	Rhyl	11.00amby bus	SX		
11.42am	Denbigh				
	RELIEVE 10.25am from Chester Turn 30 at 11.55am		SX		
	Denbigh	12.05pm Pass	SX		(6B/10)
12.19pm	Ruthin	12.25	Pass	SX	
12.41	Denbigh				
	CHANGE FOOTPLATES with 12.06pm Frt SX from Nannerch Turn 88 at 12.41pm				
	Denbigh	12.55	Frt	SX	(6B/10)
1.15	Ruthin				
1.15	SHUNT (FRT)	2.45		SX	
	Ruthin	3.00	Pass	SX	
3.14	Denbigh				
	RELIEF 3.15pm for 4.15pm pass. to Mold SX by 6B Turn 40				
	RELIEVE 12.20pm from Corwen SX Turn 121 at 3.30pm				
3.30	SHUNT (FRT)	6.00		SX	(60)
	Denbigh	6.05	LE Cpld SX		
6.30	Rhyl M. P. D.				

RHYL Turn 27

		Book On a.m.	Book Off p.m.	H. M.	
		10.40	6.05	7.25	
	Rhyl	11.00am By bus	SO		
11.42am	Denbigh		SO		
	RELIEVE 11.55am ECS to Mold Turn 87 at 11.50am		SO		(4)
	Denbigh	11.55	ECS	SO	
12.25pm	Mold	12.55pm Pass	SO		
1.32	Denbigh				
	CHANGE FOOTPLATES with 12.25pm pass SO from Ruthin Turn 31 at 1.35pm				
	Denbigh	4.00	Pass	SO	(6B/10)
4.14	Ruthin	4.40	Pass	SO	
4.54	Denbigh				
	RELIEF 4.45pm for 5.00pm Chester by Turn 33				
	Denbigh	5.00	By bus	SO	
5.45	Rhyl				

RHYL Turn 28

		Book On a. m.	Book Off p. m.	H. M.	
		4. 30	12.59	8.29	
	ENGINE PREPARED by Turn 19		SX		
	Rhyl M. P. D.	4.45am LE Cpld	SX		
-	Rhyl	5.15	Cpld Frt	SX	(6A/8)
5.40am	Denbigh	6.15	Pass	SX	
7.36	Chester	9.02	Pass	SX	
10.17	Denbigh	10.20	Pcls	SX	
10.36	Ruthin	10.45	LE	SX	
11.00	Denbigh				
11.00	SHUNT (FRT)			SX	
	RELIEF 11.55am for Shunt by Turn 50			SX	
	Denbigh	12.03pm By bus	SX		
12.44pm	Rhyl				

RHYL
Turn 30

		Book On a.m.	Book Off p.m.	H. M.
		4. 30	12.59	8. 29
	ENGINE PREPARED by Turn 35 (MO), 84 (MSX)			
	Rhyl M. P. D.	4.45am LE Cpld SX		(6B/10)
-	Rhyl	5.15	E.F .(D) SX	
5.40am	Denbigh	6.05	Pass SX	
6.19	Ruthin	6.40	Pass SX	
8.10	Chester	10.25	Pass SX	
11.42	Denbigh			
	RELIEF 11.55am for Ruthin by Turn 26			
	Denbigh	12.03pm By bus SX		
12.44pm	Rhyl			

RHYL
Turn 33

		Book On p.m.	Book Off p.m.	
		3.40	11.33	7.53
	Rhyl	4.00pm By bus SO		
4.42pm	Denbigh			
	RELIEVE 4.40pm from Ruthin		SO	
	Turn 27 at 4.54pm			
	Denbigh	5.00pm Pass	SO	(6B/10)
6.11pm	Chester	8.50	Pass SO	
10.05	Denbigh	10.10	Pass SO	
10.24	Ruthin	10.35	ECS SO	
10.48	Denbigh	10.53	L.E. SO	
11.18	Rhyl M.P.D.			

RHYL
Turn 38

		Book On p.m.	Book Off a.m.	H. M.
		4. 02	12.18	8. 16
	Rhyl	4.17pm As pass SX		
4.56pm	Chester			
	RELIEVE 4.30pm LE from Chester M.P.D.			
	6G Turn 130 at 5.05pm		SX	
	Chester	5.42pm Pass	SX	(6A/8)
7.17pm	Ruthin	7.30	Pass SX	
8.59	Chester			
	RELIEF 9.00pm for M.P.D. by 6A Turn 324 SX			
	TAKE TO ENGINE left on Turntable Road SX			
	Turntable Road.	10*25 LE	SX	
-	Chester	10.45	Pass SX	(6J/7)
11.48	Rhyl	-	LE SX	
12.03am	Rhyl M. P. D.			
		* 10.00pm S.H.		

RHYL
Turn 48

		Book On p.m.	Book Off a.m.	H. M.
		4. 40	12. 04	7. 24
	Rhyl	4.55pm As pass SO		
5.45pm	Chester			
	RELIEVE 2.35pm from Barmouth		SO	
	6A Turn 883 at 6.05pm			
	Chester	- LE	SO	(89B/4)
6.25	Chester M. P. D.			
	LEAVE ENGINE			

PREPARE ENGINE FOR	**Turn**	**Leaves M.P.D.**	
11.45pm Holyhead	6A/159	10.40pm "L"	SO
RELIEVE 7.30pm from Manchester			SO
6A Turn 314 at 8.52pm			

	Chester	9.03	Pass SO	(6J/7)
10.14	Llandudno Junction	11.05	ECS SO	
11.34	Rhyl	-	LE SO	
11.49	Rhyl M. P. D.			

RHYL
Turn 39

		Book On a.m.	Book Off p.m.	H. M.
		11. 18	5. 41	6. 23 **A**
		11.18	6.38	7. 20 **B**

PREPARE ENGINE FOR:	**Turn**	**Leaves M. P. D.**	
1.40pm Mold Junction	97	1.10pm "L" SO	

	RELIEVE 11.20am from Chester			
	Turn 33 at 12.23pm			
	Rhyl	12.36pm Pass	SO	(26F/12)
1.53pm	Bangor	3.25	LE SO}	**A**- To 14th Oct
3.55	Llandudno Junction M.P.D.		}	& commencing
			}	14th April
	LEAVE ENGINE		}	
	Llandudno Junction	4.58	As pass or }	
5.02	Rhyl		as required }	
1.53pm	Bangor	-	LE SO}	**B** - 21st Oct. to
1.58	Bangor M. P. D.		}	7th April incl
	COAL		}	
	Bangor M. P. D.	5.15	LE SO}	
-	Bangor	5.30 Cpld Pass	SO}	
5.49pm	Llandudno Junction		}	
	RELIEF 5.50pm for Chester by 6G Turn 137 SO}			
	Llandudno Junction	5.55	As pass orSO}	
6.23	Rhyl		as required }	

RHYL
Turn 60

ONE CLASS 3F (Mid. 0-6-0)

	Rhyl M. P. D.	6.00am LE	SX	(34)(6B/244)
6.30am	Denbigh			
	SHUNT (FRT)	8.05	SX	
	Denbigh	8.10	Frt SX	(121)
8.30	Ruthin			
8.30	SHUNT (FRT)	9.00	SX	
	Ruthin	9.00	Frt SX	
10.42	Corwen	12.20pm Frt	SX	
2.15	Denbigh			
3.40	SHUNT (FRT)	6.00	SX	(26)
	Denbigh	6.05	LE Cpld. SX	
6.30	Rhyl M. P. D.			

RHYL
Turn 72

ENGINE AND MEN'S WORKINGS

		Book On a.m.	Book Off p.m.	H. M.
		5. 40	1. 45	8. 05

ONE CLASS 3 (L. & Y. 0-6-0)

	ENGINE PREPARED by Turn 19 (MO), 6B Turn 244 MSX			
	Rhyl M. P. D.	5.55am LE	SX	
-	Rhyl			
6.00am	SHUNT (FRT)	10.25	SX	
10.25	SHUNT (MIXED)	1.25pm	SX	
	RELIEF 1.25pm for Shunt by Turn 73			
	(Also works 9.30am Trip to Roberts & Lanes Coal Sidings) SX			

RHYL
Turn 74

		Book On a.m.	Book Off a.m.	H. M.
		3. 10	11. 10	8. 00

PREPARE ENGINE FOR	**Turn**	**Leaves M.P.D.**	
6. 00am Chester	35	5.30am "L" SO	
		5. 00am S.H.	
7.15am Bangor	37	6.45am "L" SO	
		6.30am S.H.	

	Rhyl M. P. D.	5.55am LE	SO	
-	Rhyl			
6.00am	SHUNT (FRT)	10.50	SO	
	(Also works 9.30am trip to Roberts & Lanes Coal Sidings) SO			
	RELIEF 10.50am for Shunt by Turn 75	SO		

RHYL
Turn 85

		Book On a.m.	Book Off p.m.	H.M.	
		4.15	12.15	8.00	MO
		3.50	12.30	8.40	MSX
			a.m.		
		2.50	10.50	8.00	SO

RELIEVE 1.40am (MX) 2.16am (MO) T.F. D
from Mold Junction
6B Turns 243 and 244 at 4.35am (MO)
4.10am (MSX) 3.10am (SO)

-	Rhyl	4.40am	T.F.	MO	(6B/101)
	Rhyl	4.15	T.F.	MX	(6B/126)
6.30am	Llandudno Junction	-	Loco Coal	MX	
6.35	Llandudno Junction M.P.D.				
	Llandudno Junction	8.15	LE	MSO	
8.50am	Rhyl M.P.D.				
	PREPARE FRESH ENGINE			MSX	
	Llandudno Junction M.P.D.	9.18	LE	MSX	
	Llandudno Junction	9.38	Cpld Frt	MSX	(6G/239)
9.53am	Penmaenmawr	10.20	E.F.(E)	MSX	
10.37	Llandudno Junction				

RELIEF 10.37am for Chester by 6B Turn 221 MSX
TAKE TO FRESH ENGINE PREPARED
by 6G Turn 319   MSX

	Llandudno Junction M.P.D.	11.15	LE	MSX	(6B/126)
1.55	Rhyl				

RELIEF 12.10pm for 1.00pm Mold Junction
by Turn 82   MSX

PREPARE ENGINE FOR Turn Leaves M.P.D.
1.00pm Mold Junction	82	12.30pm "L"	MO
M.P.D. Duties		(12.05pm)	MO
		(10.40am)	SO

RHYL
DENBIGH RESIDENTIAL MEN
Turn 121

		Book On a.m.	Book Off p.m.	H.M.	
		7.40	3.40	8.00	

	RELIEVE Frt. Shunt Turn 34 (MO)			SX	
	6B Turn 244				
7.50am	SHUNT (FRT)	8.05am		SX	(60)
	Denbigh	8.10am	Frt	SX	
8.30am	Ruthin				
	SHUNT (FRT)	9.00		SX	
	Ruthin	9.00	Frt	SX	
10.42	Corwen	12.20pm	Frt	SX	
2.15pm	Denbigh				

RELIEF 3.30pm for SHUNT (FRT) by Turn 26 SX

RHYL
DENBIGH RESIDENTIAL MEN
Turn 122

		Book On p.m.	Book Off p.m.	H.M.	
		3.00	11.05	8.05	

	RELIEVE 1.35pm Pass from Chester				
	6B Turn 40 at 3.10pm			SX	
	Denbigh	3.22pm	Pass	SX	(6B/10)
4.37pm	Chester	6.35	Pass	SX	
8.09	Ruthin	8.25	Pass	SX	
8.39	Denbigh	8.45	ECS	SX	
9.07	Rhyl	-	LE	SX	
9.22	Rhyl M.P.D.				
	LEAVE ENGINE				
	Rhyl	10.05	by bus	SX	
10.50	Denbigh				

Rhyl M.P.D. 1958. Locomotives out of steam in the shed yard included L&Y 0-6-0 No.**52119**, Fowler Class 4F No.**44367** and L&Y 0-6-0 No.**52432**. The portable coal loader protrudes into the picture. Notice the coal, clinker and assorted hardware littering the yard.
Huw Edwards.

The Welsh Dragon

(upper). **Rhyl. August 1952.** Reference has already been made to 'The Welsh Dragon' pull & push train that ran between Rhyl and Llandudno in the summer months. Here the unit draws into the Up side Bay platform. Notice the headboard, complete with a partly obscured 'red dragon' symbol uppermost. *Gordon Coltas*

(centre). **Rhyl. August 1952.** Motive power for 'The Welsh Dragon' was provided by Ivatt 2-6-2MT with vacuum control equipment installed. The driver was able to control the regulator from the cab of the trailer car, but the locomotives had to be suitably modified accordingly. They could be easily identified by the square steam pipes from the smokebox, the smokebox modifications on either side and the twin sets of vacuum pipes as well as the steam heater pipes. Here, nearly new No.**41320** stands at the head of the three coach formation awaiting the next trip to Llandudno, in No.1 bay.
Gordon Coltas

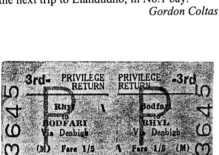

(lower). **Rhyl. August 1952.** Usually 'The Welsh Dragon' operated from No.1 bay on the Up side, but the first working of the day pulled into No.2 platform, after collecting the stock from the carriage shed. A freight from Mold Junction to Llandudno Junction trundles past on the Down Fast line, whilst a guard makes his way across the tracks, perhaps to work the motor train. *Gordon Coltas*

(upper). **Rhyl. n.d.** Rhyl suffered the disadvantage of having only one main Up platform and consequently when the station was rebuilt, was made as wide as possible, to cater for large numbers of passengers who would hopefully be entrained in as short a time as possible. The western (Llandudno) end also contained No.1 bay, which was under-used, apart from 'The Welsh Dragon' or some of the workings off the Vale of Clwyd line. A single siding was used for parking coaching stock for short periods of time between workings.

V.R. Anderson.

(centre). **Rhyl. August 1952.** Ex L&Y 0-6-0 No.**52356** waits at the shed yard throat on the Up side. Notice the advert for the North Wales Weekly Runabout ticket at 16/6d or 82½p in current money. For seven days one could travel from Holyhead to Rhyl and along most of the former LMS branch lines. *Gordon Coltas*

(lower). **Rhyl. c.1951.** Stanier 2-6-0 No.**42975** of Mold Junction (6B) shed stands at the head of the C490 working which was the 11.35am (Saturdays Only) from Newcastle-upon-Tyne to Llandudno, due Rhyl 5.10pm and comprised of mixed passenger stock, at the Down platform. Stock for the 5.20pm to Denbigh along the Vale of Clwyd line stands across the platform in the bay, awaiting its motive power which came off the shed. *Author's collection*

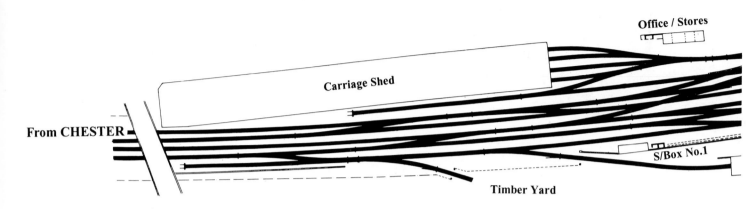

Office / Stores

Carriage Shed

From CHESTER

S/Box No.1

Timber Yard

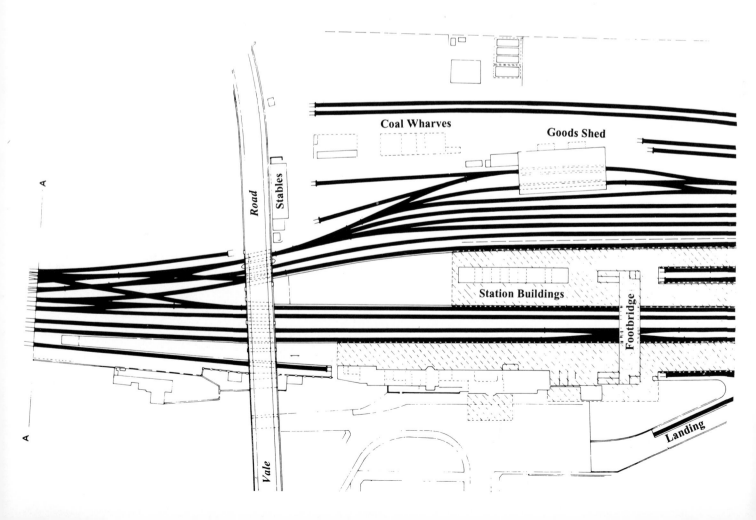

Coal Wharves

Goods Shed

Road

Stables

Station Buildings

Footbridge

Landing

Vale

Rhyl. c.1955. 'Royal Scot' Class 4-6-0 No.**46166** *London Rifle Brigade* of Crewe North (5A) shed crosses from the Down Fast to the Down Slow at the eastern end of the station with a ten coach working from Euston to Bangor. On the right of the picture is the four road carriage shed. The Up Fast starter is pulled off. In the middle distance is Rhyl No.1 box, still operational and subject to a preservation order also covering the entire station. Over the fence can be seen the body of a coach serving as a store, now sadly gone. The trackwork has now been 'rationalised' and the goods yard, carriage sidings and shed have long gone.

K. Field.

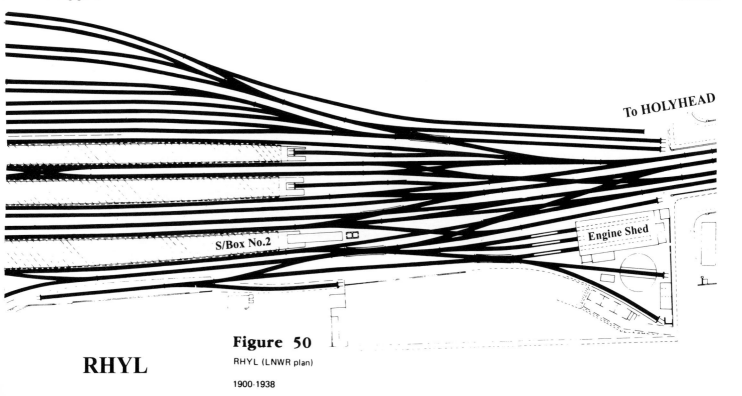

Figure 50

RHYL

RHYL (LNWR plan)

1900-1938

(upper). **Rhyl. 14th September 1967.** The Down passenger loop was a gloomy area of the station, and the wind screens, placed to prevent the worst excesses of the weather from affecting passengers, merely adds to the claustrophobic effect under a dark all-over canopy. Out of season it was used infrequently, only trains that spent some time standing for mail or newspaper traffic using it with any regularity. The gas lamps are still in use at the time this view was taken.
British Railways
London Midland Region.

(lower). **Rhyl. 9th May 1949.** Until the Ivatt 2-6-2T locomotives became more widely available, pull& push, or motor trains, were worked with vintage tank engines, in the case of the Western Division of the former LMS, Webb 0-6-2T, suitably modified with vacuum control equipment. Here, No.**58889** sporting a Rhyl (7D) shed plate, stands in the Denbigh bay at the western end of the Down platform after working the 10.10am from Denbigh. Earlier in the year it had spent some time at Crewe works, awaiting a decision on its future, but was subsequently overhauled and returned to traffic without having acquired the new 'Ferret and Dartboard' crest,Fortunately for Rhyl men, it was transferred to Abergavenny in December 1950, and its departure was not mourned by many.   *E.S. Russell.*

(upper).**Rhyl. n.d.** The need for segregation on the station footbridge was paramount during heavy seasonal periods. This massive structure (No.77 on the Chester to Holyhead line) was constructed with two passageways, one served by lifts, the other by stairs, although the latter, used by pedestrians, was further adapted by use of the chains shown here. The bridge consisted of wrought iron columns and plate girders - the outer members having glazed sections above the parapet - wrought iron flights and patent (oak) block steps, a feature surviving to this day, having given close on 100 years of service.

V.R. Anderson

(lower). **Rhyl. 14th September 1967.** A detail of part of the main Up, or No.1 platform. The wide platform was necessary especially on summer Saturdays, when crowds awaiting trains would be packed solid, and indeed were obliged to queue outside the station. This view beneath the vast canopy protecting No.1.platform shows the fabric of the station following enlargement at the turn of the century. With the exception of the enamel signs, Wymans Bookstall and other peripherals, the scene is still very much as set by the LNWR. The superficial brickwork gave a uniform look to the station buildings but unfortunately somewhat reduced the effect of the main entrance, a fine example of one of Francis Thompson's station designs for the Chester and Holyhead Railway, now happily subject to a preservation order. The station seats, again emphasizing their parenthood, were based on designs dating from 1872. *British Railways London Midland Region.*

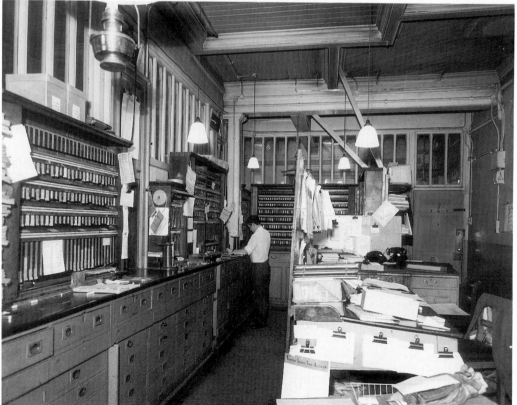

(upper). **Rhyl. 14th September 1967.** The booking office exterior, inside the station foyer presented the traditional appearance for LNWR designed stations, with separate windows for Up and Down direction passengers. The third (nearest) window would be pressed into use when queues built up and delays to trains might ensue. Notice the chalk board for 'latest information' to the travelling public, easier to digest than the tannoy announcements.

British Railways
London Midland Region

(lower). **Rhyl. 14th September 1967.** The traditional ticket office interior, with rows of Edmondson type tickets, oil and electric lamps, telephones, ticket stamping presses, and current traffic notices held in clips. Not a computerised ticket issuing machine in sight!

British Railways
London Midland Region.

(upper) **Rhyl. n.d.** The main entrance to Rhyl station was protected by a large canopy that gave some protection to passengers and enabled taxi fares to remain in the dry, unless they had to join a queue to book tickets. In the peak summer season, taxis did a roaring trade and it was in the railway's own interests that the foyer was kept as clear as possible. Notice also the array of cars including a post war (1948) Austin 16, probably a private taxi; a pre-war Morris 8 van, possibly a Rover 16 and a pre-war Bedford 3 ton van. Any one of these vehicles offered for sale today would fetch very respectable sums of money for their owner.   *British Railways London Midland Region.*

Rhyl.1956. Developments in Rhyl around the turn of the century resulted in this range of buildings on the Up side. The decorative style of brickwork enabled the new buildings to blend in with the existing structures provided by Thompson for the Chester & Holyhead Railway, seen here to the extreme right of the picture. At the time of the photograph, rail travel to and from Rhyl was enjoying an 'Indian Summer' as the posters suggest. The seasonal traffic which had caused the station's prominence subsequently ebbed away to reduce its status and size. Nowadays, two platforms suffice for the business on offer. Forthcoming proposals envisage a return to a bus/rail interchange in the station forecourt.

British Rail.

Rhyl. c. June 1956. The station exterior, somewhat overshadowed by the Crosville presence, on a not untypical summer's day, the soaking forecourt, ensuring that passengers off the trains did not hang about. The double decker centre picture was brand new, having been taken into service only the previous month. Several factors give this away, namely the highly polished paintwork, the thin cream band between the lower and upper decks, which was painted out at the first visit to the works for overhaul. The Company's Fleet Number, MG807, which was superseded in 1958 by the more familiar code 'DLG' for the Gardner engined Bristol 'Lodekka' models. Note also the old Route Number - 409, Rhyl to Colwyn Bay, replaced by a different system in late 1958. The poster on the back of the bus proclaims that the Royal Welsh Show was to take place at Rhyl on July 25/6/7th 1956. A Stand Inspector, complete with company issue mackintosh and flat hat is just visible between the buses and whose job under these adverse conditions was not envied. The single decker was a Bristol LL6B model, new in 1952, staffed by student conductor, clad in civvies, complete with cash bag and Setright ticket machine making for the platform door. Notice the stand signs, advising passengers to 'Queue Here for Buses to ....' Vast quantities of passengers were shifted every day, whilst every Saturday in the season would see horrendous queues of people waiting to board buses to Winkup's Camp and the like and it was not unusual for passengers to wait an hour before they were finally able to board the bus. Those were the days, when most buses were staffed by a driver and conductor, and one-man operated forward entrance vehicles were only found on the most rural routes. *V.R. Anderson.*

Rhyl. 3rd June 1963. Rebuilt Royal Scot Class 4-6-0 No.**46149** *The Middlesex Regiment* attached to Manchester Longsight (9A) shed awaits departure time at the eastern end of Rhyl station with a return excursion to Birmingham. For several years this was a Holyhead engine and a familiar sight on the North Wales coast workings. *A. Tyson*

Coach Working

The coach working on the Denbigh, Ruthin & Corwen, and Vale of Clwyd lines has already been dealt with in *Scenes From the Past 15: The Denbigh and Mold Line* when the relevant extracts from The *Diagram of Coach Working* dated September 1925 was specified. It must be pointed out that coach working diagrams listed covered all the passenger traffic working through Denbigh, and no set of stock worked exclusively on any one line in the district, although this did occur elsewhere. It would be pointless in repeating the 1925 information here, and consequently the examples given below are taken from the Summer 1933 edition.

Coach Working Diagrams were prepared and issued timed to coincide with the introduction of each new working time table, a procedure adopted by most railway companies. The LMS Western Division merely continued with the practice started by the LNWR, keeping to the same format. Nevertheless, after ten years, and during a recession which inhibited railway business, the LMS were anxious to make economies. It was decided that after the September 1933 Diagram of Coach Working had been issued, the publication would be discontinued, although in practice, the information and circuits were prepared as formerly. The diagrams were subsequently prepared on duplicated paper, and it is not known whether any complete set survived.

For this reason it was decided that the Summer 1933 diagrammed working that worked over the lines was worthy of inclusion, and readers familiar with the 1925 circuits can make comparisons. It should be pointed out that some of the coding may appear obscure, but these are explained within each circuit set details.

All the regular coaching stock working over the lines through Denbigh was designated as part of the **Llandudno District** (Circuit Nos 819 to 832) which comprised two non-corridor vehicles, tare weight 50 tons, which had replaced the earlier six-wheel stock **Strengthening Sets** (Nos 843 to 857), and No.871 a **Motor Set**. made up of two vehicles. In the fullness of time, the ex LNWR non corridor bogie coaches which formed the Llandudno District sets were replaced by LMS non corridor stock, which were replaced in due course by modern steel panelled non corridor stock. There was no through coach working on or off the line to; all working being local by nature, although the sets worked to the Wirral and Whitchurch as part of their circuit. The practice of displaying the circuit and district set numbers was abandoned around 1930 although this practice was maintained by other companies.

It should be borne in mind that the circuit diagrams represented the normal working stock, and did not include excursion traffic, which could comprise most types of passenger carrying vehicles. It was not unknown for G.W.R. or L.N.E.R. stock to work over the lines during the summer season, but such occasions were comparatively rare, and most excursion workings before and after the Second World War would have been made up of LMS stock. Such workings were prepared by the Divisional Rolling Stock office, who printed a booklet published at Easter and then weekly during the period from Whitsuntide to September, with a final edition for Christmas week. These were known as the R.S.D. booklets, and would give the stock allocated to each special working a clause number, specifying the make-up, weight and relevant timing points. Details of timings would be provided in the Programmes of Special Trains, published weekly throughout the year, and supplied to all Traffic Staff.

LLANDUDNO DISTRICT SETS

No.819. Worked by No.823 (M) and No.823 (MO).

			arr	dep	
			a.m.	p.m.	
Chester	...	...	...	7.32	A.
Denbigh	...	...	8.47	9.10	A.
Corwen	...	...	10.01	10.55	B.
			p.m.	p.m.	
Chester	...	...	1.08	2.30	SO C.
Shotton	...	...	2.45	4.05	SO. C.
Chester	...	...	4.22	6.05	SO
Whitchurch	...	...	6.53	9.10	SO
Chester	...	...	9.49		

    A - R extra Corwen

    B - N extra Road Van for Rhyl from Ruthin to Denbigh (S).

    C - 2 F

Works No.825 (M), and No.825 (MO).

No.820. Worked by No.827 (M) and No.827 (MO).

			arr	dep	
			a.m.	a.m.	
Denbigh	...	...	...	6.43	A.
Corwen	...	...	7.45	8.08	A.
Denbigh	...	...	8.58	9.02	A.
Rhyl	...	...	9.27	9.50	
Denbigh	...	...	10.21	10.50	
Rhyl	...	...	11.16	11.50	
			p.m.	p.m.	
Denbigh	...	...	12.21	12.28	SO
Rhyl	...	...	12.54	...	
Denbigh	...	...	...	12.40	S
Rhyl	...	...	1.06	1.20	
Denbigh	...	...	1.48	2.33	
Rhyl	...	...	3.09	3.37	
Denbigh	...	...	4.08	5.00	
Chester	...	...	6.09	6.50	
Denbigh	...	...	8.05	8.10	
Ruthin	...	...	8.23	9.00	
Denbigh	...	...	9.16	9.25	B.
Rhyl	...	...	9.51	10.25	C.
Denbigh	...	...	10.53		

    A - 3 N extra

    B - Double (S)

    C - 2 N

Works No.829 (M) and No.829 (MO).

No.821. Worked by No.821 (FO), No.824 (ThO)
No.822 (TWSO) and No.825 (MO).

			arr	dep	
			a.m.	a.m.	
Mold	...	...	...	9.11	ThO
Chester	...	...	9.38	...	\
Denbigh	...	...	...	9.06	MTh
				p.m.	
Chester	...	...	10.09	1.12	A
			p.m.		
Denbigh	...	...	2.27	2.30	A
Ruthin	...	...	2.42	4.30	A
Denbigh	...	...	4.46	4.55	A. C.
Rhyl	...	...	5.22	6.10	A.
Denbigh	...	...	6.39	6.41	
Ruthin	...	...	6.53	7.08	
Denbigh	...	...	7.24	7.35	A.
Rhyl	...	...	8.00	8.35	A.
Denbigh	...	...	9.03	9.20	B.
Ruthin	...	...	9.33	10.20	WThSO
Denbigh	...	...	10.36		

    A - 3 N

    B - LK (S)

    C - To be made up to 6 (ThSO)

Works No.822 (TWSO), No.821 (FO), No.827 (ThO) and No.827 (MO)

No.822. Worked by No.821 (TWSO), No.822 (ThFO)
and No.828 (MO).

			arr a.m.	dep a.m.	
Ruthin	...	...	...	6.58	C. D.
Denbigh	...	...	7.14	7.18	D.
				p.m.	
Chester	...	...	8.31	1.00	A. B.
			p.m.		
Birkenhead	...	...	1.47	2.20	A. B.
West Kirby	...	...	3.15	3.25	A. B.
Birkenhead	...	...	4.25	4.43	A. B.
Chester	...	...	5.25	6.05	B.
Denbigh	...	...	7.12	8.10	
Rhyl	...	...	8.35	9.25	E.
Denbigh	...	...	9.55	10.00	**ThO**
Ruthin	...	...	10.14		
Denbigh	...	...	...	10.00	**WSO**
Corwen	...	...	10.50	11#10	**WSO**
Ruthin	...	...	11.32	12#00 night	**SO**
Denbigh	...	...	12.12am		

    A - 2 F (SO)
    B - LK (S), double (SO) To be made up equal 11.
    C - R Chester off 5.20am from Rhyl
    D - N extra
    E - 2 N
       # - Empty Stock Train
Works No.822 (ThFO), No.821 (TWSO) and No.823 (MO).

No.823. Worked by No.828 (M) and No.822 (MO)

			arr a.m.	dep a.m.	
Denbigh	...	...	...	7.40	A.
Ruthin	...	...	7.54	8.05	G
Denbigh	...	...	8.23	8.32	G. B.
Chester	...	...	9.38	10.25	B
			p.m.	p.m.	
Corwen	...	...	12.42	1.30	B. C.
Denbigh	...	...	2.14	2.17	B. D.
Chester	...	...	3.06		

    A - LK (S) rear
    B - 2 F July and September, 3 August
    C - Depart 1.37pm (FSO)
    D - Depart 2.20pm (FO), 2.24pm (SO)
      due Chester 3.08pm, (FO), 3.13pm (SO).
    E - Double, Mold to Chester (ThO)
    G - LK (S) front
Works No.819 (M) and No.819 (MO)

No.824. Worked by No.825 (M) and No.824 (MO)

			arr a.m.	dep a.m.	
Rhyl	...	...	...	9.00	B.
Denbigh	...	...	9.30	9.50	B.
Rhyl	...	...	10.16	10.50	B.
Denbigh	...	...	11.21	11.50	B.
			p.m.	p.m.	
Rhyl	...	...	12.16	1.20	B.
Denbigh	...	...	1.48	3.30	
Chester	...	...	4.44	5.15	A.
Denbigh	...	...	6.20	8.10	**SO**
Rhyl	...	...	8.35		
Denbigh	...	...	...	10.00	**ThO**
Mold	...	...	10.37		

    A - LK (S) in front
    B - 2 N
Works No.827 (MTh)., No.821 (ThO) and No.824 (MO).

No.825. Worked by No.819 (M) and No.819 (MO)

			arr a.m.	dep a.m.	
Chester	...	...	...	9.00	
Denbigh	...	...	10.15	10.25	A.
				p.m.	
Ruthin	...	...	10.39	12.38	
			p.m.		
Denbigh	...	...	12.54	12.58	
Chester	...	...	1.52	2.18	A. B.
Denbigh	...	...	3.22	3.30	B.
Corwen	...	...	4.19	5.00	B.
Chester	...	...	7.10	8.03	
Denbigh	...	...	9.18	10.00	**SO**
Chester	...	...	11.12		
Denbigh	...	...	...	9.25	**S**
Rhyl	...	...	9.51		

    A - 2.15pm (SO)
Works No.824 (M) and No.821 (MO).

No.827. Worked by No.824 (MTh), No.821 (ThO) and No.821 (MO)

			arr p.m.	dep p.m.	
Denbigh	...	...	...	1.30	A.
Rhyl	...	...	2.00	2.30	B.
Denbigh	...	...	3.04	3.37	B.
Rhyl	...	...	4.08	4.25	B.
Denbigh	...	...	4.55	5.12	B.
Corwen	...	...	6.07	6.50	B.
Chester	...	...	9.02	9.25	
Denbigh	10.40				

    A - BB
    B - 2 N July and September, 3 August.
Works No.820 (M) and No.820 (MO).

No.828. Worked by No.829 (M) and No.829 (MO)

			arr a.m.	dep a.m.	
Denbigh	...	...	...	7.45	E.
Rhyl	...	...	8A17	8.30	E.
Denbigh	...	...	8.58	9.06	D. E.
Chester	...	...	10.09	10.25	C. E.
				p.m.	
Birkenhead (W)	...		11.13	3.12	C. E.
			p.m.		
Chester	...	...	3.58	4.25	B. E.
Denbigh	...	...	5.40	5.50	E. G.
Rhyl	...	...	6.15	7.10	E.
Denbigh	...	...	7.38	7.50	E.
Corwen	...	...	8.39	9.10	E.
Denbigh	...	...	9.55	10.05	E.
Rhyl	...	...	10.27	11.10	E
Denbigh	...	...	11.38	11.40	**ThSO**
				night	
Ruthin	...	...	11.54	12#00	**ThO**
			a.m.		
Denbigh	...	...	12#12		

    A - 8.12am (SO)
    B - R Lime Street to Mold
    C - (SO) vehicles from G.W. Line due
    Chester 9.12am attached front. Alsao conveys
    L.M.S. K (S), 2 N (SO).
    D - Double (MTh)
    E - 2 N
    G - To be 6 (ThSO)
    # - Empty Stock Train
Works No.823 (M) and No.822 (MO)
